Theory of Education

14 March 2010   Athens

Joe & Diane,

    With very best wishes and thanks.

    Yours,
    David & Lippita

Theory of Education

David A. Turner

continuum
LONDON • NEW YORK

Continuum International Publishing Group
The Tower Building
11 York Road
London
SE1 7NX

15 East 26th Street
New York, NY 10010

First published 2004
The paperback edition published 2005

© David A.Turner 2004

All rights reserved. No part of this publication may be reproduced or transmitted in any form or by any means, electronic or mechanical, including photocopying, recording, or any information storage or retrieval system, without prior permission in writing from the publishers.

British Library Cataloguing-in-Publication Data
A catalogue record for this book is available from the British Library.

ISBN: 08264 7257 5 (hardback)
        08264 8709 2 (paperback)

Library of Congress Cataloguing-in-Publication Data
A catalogue record for this book is available from the Library of Congress.

Typeset by 4alldesigns
Printed and bound in Great Britain by Cromwell Press, Trowbridge, Wiltshire

CONTENTS

List of Figures   vii

Acknowledgements   ix

CHAPTER ONE:

STUCK IN THE MUD WITH THE WHEELS SPINNING   1

CHAPTER TWO: CLEARING THE GROUND   15
Laws and Scientific Method   16
Game Theory Models   25

CHAPTER THREE:

LARGE SCALE STATISTICAL SURVEY METHODS   35
Statistical Methods   35
From Description to Policy   45

CHAPTER FOUR:

ACTION RESEARCH   53
A Critique of Scientific Method   53
The Implications of the Critique   59

CHAPTER FIVE:

POSTMODERNISM   67
'Theory' as a range of activities   68
Theory as the search for abstract generalisations   69
Theory as opposed to creativity   71

CHAPTER SIX:

GAME THEORY AND INDIVIDUAL CHOICE IN
SCHOOLING   77
Game Theory and Policy   78
Two Person Zero Sum Games   82
Games Against Nature   85
Mixed Strategies   91

CHAPTER SEVEN:

LINEAR PROGRAMMING AND SOCIOLOGICAL LAWS   99
Sociological Laws   101
Planning Decisions in a School   105
Attainability and Sustainability   112

CHAPTER EIGHT:

LINEAR PROGRAMMING AND EDUCATIONAL POLICY 123
A Rule Governed Funding System   124
Impact of the Rules on Different Institutions   131
Overall Policy Objectives and Policy Instruments   138

CHAPTER NINE:

GROUP DECISION MAKING   143
A Model Classroom   144
Arrow's Impossibility Theorem   147
Muddling Towards a Policy   155

CHAPTER TEN:

CHAOS AND COMPLEXITY   161
Emergence and Iteration   165
Feedback Loops   167
Unpredictability   170
Sensitivity to Initial Conditions, or The Butterfly Effect   171
Complexity and Management   174
Complexity and a Reassertion of Values   179

CHAPTER ELEVEN:

CONCLUSIONS   185
Modernism   187
Critique of Modernism   190
Postmodernism   191
Concluding Remarks   193

References: 197

Index   203

List of Figures

Figure 2.1: Hooke's Law   18
Figure 2.2: A pay-off matrix for the game of Chicken   26
Figure 2.3: Pay-off matrix for Twins   27
Figure 3.1: William Blake's portrait of Newton   37
Figure 3.2: Handicapping Yacht Race Times   38
Figure 6.1: Simple pay-off matrix for a zero–sum game.   82
Figure 6.2: Pay off matrix for modified game of Mora   83
Figure 6.3: A linear programming interpretation of the modified game
of Mora   84
Figure 6.4: Fisherman's game against Nature   86
Figure 6.5: General Matrix for Game against Nature   87
Figure 6.6: Pay off matrix for middle-class boys   88
Figure 7.1: The operating conditions of a transistor   101
Figure 7.2: A point in the policy space   106
Figure 7.3: A budgetary constraint   107
Figure 7.4: A minimum staffing budget   109
Figure 7.5: A minimum expenditure on upkeep   110
Figure 7.6: Constraints and an area of attainable policies.   111
Figure 7.7: A point which is both attainable and sustainable.   114
Figure 7.8: A point which is attainable but not sustainable   115
Figure 8.1: Recruitment Policy Space   125
Figure 8.2: The lower boundary of the policy space   126
Figure 8.3: A moderation line (after Pratt and Hillier)   128
Figure 8.4: The upper boundary of the policy space   129
Figure 8.5: Attainable policies   131
Figure 8.6: Comparison of institutions of the same size   132
Figure 8.7: Area of sustainable policy   135
Figure 8.8: Bidding for "cash recovery"   138
Figure 9.1: A Multi-Person Game of Classroom Discipline   144
Figure 9.2: Preferences in a Group of Three People   147
Figure 10.1: Part of the Mandelbrot Set   165
Figure 10.2: A small part of Figure 10.1 magnified many hundreds of
times   167
Figure 10.3: A Fractal as a Representation of Nature   169
Figure 10.4: The Lorenz Attractor   171

Acknowledgements

One way and another, this book has been more than 30 years in the making. Even if I were to try to remember all of those people who have contributed to it, and to record what they have done, I do not think that I would come close to acknowledging all of the debts that are due. Members of my family, colleagues, teachers and students have all contributed at different times and in different ways. Some, particularly close friends and colleagues know that they have contributed, because they have read draft material and have provided helpful comments on it. Others may not even know that they have contributed, as when students have shown an interest in the issues that have interested me. That disinterested commentary on what might be good topics for inclusion has been particularly helpful.

From all that list of people to whom I owe acknowledgement, I therefore pick out only two for special mention. My wife, Guadalupe, has provided support longest and most over the production of this work in all its various aspects. And Helen Evans turned countless audio tapes into organised typescript. Without either of these contributions, the present book would have been impossible.

As to the rest, I hope that individuals who have contributed in other ways will recognise themselves under the general rubric, and accept my thanks.

CHAPTER ONE: STUCK IN THE MUD WITH THE WHEELS SPINNING

In 2003 a report on the condition of social science research came to two apparently conflicting conclusions: that a large and growing body of research in the social services is being conducted in the UK, and that criticism of the quality of research is also growing (Commission on the Social Sciences, 2003). Similar debates can also be found in the USA.

My purpose in this book is to examine the criticisms which have been made of the quality of research in Education Studies. I do not wish to stop, however, with the presentation of criticism. If a critique of current research in Education Studies was my goal, this book would end after Chapter 5. I wish to go beyond criticism, to show the directions in which that critique of research is pointing, and to give at least some indication of what better research could look like.

Since 1995 there has been a growing debate which reflects concern about the quality of educational research. In the UK an important contribution to that debate was the report presented to Ofsted by Tooley (1998). The publication of that report was followed by an extensive debate conducted within the British Education Research Association (BERA) through the media of *Research Intelligence*, the BERA website and the addresses delivered by a number of presidents of BERA. Another strand in the debate has been the establishment of the National Educational Research Forum (NERF) which has produced a number of reports including one entitled *Quality of Educational Research* (NERF, 2000).

This debate concerning the quality of educational research is not restricted to the UK. In the USA the National Research Council has produced a report entitled *Scientific Research in Education* (Shavelson and Towne, 2002).

The main focus of the debate has not been the quality of theory in educational research. Indeed in many ways theory is seen as unproblematic. Certainly Tooley and others offer examples of poor practice in educational research but those examples are presented as illustrations of the failure to meet norms which are widely accepted and which, if properly applied, would lead to research of high quality.

For example, the NERF (2000: 2) report argues,

> "that the methodological and logical rules and procedures for social science research are well described and readily available, although naturally they differ for different types of research. It is not necessary for these to be reproduced but, to the extent that they are not universally adhered to, the research community needs to address the adequacy of research training provision, including 'continuing professional development'."

The implication is that there are clearly understood procedures for securing high quality research. Individuals are blamed for the lack of quality when their behaviour falls below standards which are supposed to be widely agreed and understood.

In this book I shall be arguing from a very different premise, namely that the methodological and logical rules and procedures currently applied in social scientific research, and particularly in educational research, are inappropriate and incapable of leading to the development of high quality educational research. I shall argue that the problems highlighted in the debate about the quality of educational research arise from a crisis of educational theory and are not aberrations on the part of individual researchers. I shall argue that in order to develop high quality educational research we need to reconsider what constitutes good educational theory and to seek ways of overcoming the current impasse. Part of this argument is a critique of current methods. But I want to go beyond mere negative reflections on the current state of educational research to indicate some possible theoretical frameworks for the development of future educational research.

Before proceeding to those examples of how educational theory might be developed, however, it would be as well to establish the need for a new direction in educational theory. That can be done by examining the key concerns which are raised in the debate about the quality of educational research.

There are two main foci of criticism of current educational research in the debate which is being conducted at present. The first relates to the way in which researchers draw upon, or fail to draw upon, the corpus of educational research which exists. The second main focus of criticism relates to the involvement, or lack of involvement, of policy makers and practitioners in research, and the impact which educational research has on practice and policy.

On the question of engaging with and building upon previous research Tooley notes that:

> "On the whole though, these research questions exposed in a dramatic way what many will consider to be a severe weakness in this strand of educational research, namely, that it does consist of researchers by and large doing their research in a vacuum unnoticed and unheeded by anyone else in their field."(Tooley, 1998: 68).

The specific criticisms which Tooley makes are that researchers do not go back to primary sources in literature, do not replicate previous studies in the field and do not critically examine theories which have been previously propounded. Tooley adds that where researchers do engage with theoretical positions within the social science literature he has identified "an especially questionable practice which we have dubbed the 'adulation' of 'great' thinkers."(Tooley, 1998: 74).

In rather less contentious terms the report of the NERF Sub-group on Research Quality suggests:

> "That in all cases research should be thoroughly and comprehensively located within relevant previous studies and literature. *The research community needs to consider whether it universally adheres to this precept".*(NERF, 2000: 2). (stress in the original)

The clear implication is that research does not always meet the standards which the NERF Sub-group would like and that much falls short in its ability to build upon previous work.

On the question of developing research which has an impact upon policy the NERF Sub-group notes that:

> "The user community needs to show a capacity and a willingness to engage with researchers and to modify practices in the light of well-founded and persuasive research, and to communicate its needs clearly. This applies to policy makers as much as to practitioners... *The user community needs to consider how far it currently fulfils its responsibilities to engage effectively with research."* (NERF, 2000: 3) - (stress in the original)

These two areas of concern highlight the fact that researchers, policy makers and practitioners find it difficult to build upon a corpus of research which exists within Education Studies. The implication of the reports by Tooley and the NERF is that this is a question of quality. They argue that, if researchers reported their methods more accurately, the details of their analyses, sample sizes and so on, then it would be possible for research to be developed in a cumulative way and for policy outcomes to be informed by research.

In contrast to this position I am going to argue that what we are witnessing is a failure to develop 'good theory' in education; in this context 'good theory' implies the development of frameworks for analyses and models which facilitate the development of cumulative research and the development of a policy making technology. From this perspective the failure of researchers, policy makers and practitioners to take up and build upon existing research frameworks is a symptom of an underlying problem with the development of theory in the area of Education Studies. Until that theoretical shortcoming is addressed directly, educational research will remain a collection of fragmented and sometimes brilliant insights into the educational process, but a body of accepted understanding of educational processes will not be developed.

Neither Tooley nor the NERF directly address the question of what constitutes good theory in educational research. Tooley describes a range of methodological practices both qualitative and quantitative, and questions whether the conclusions of studies are validly and persuasively argued within their own framework. The NERF Sub-group argues that:

> "Educational research is mainly a species of various kinds of social science research. As such it cannot be separated from the long-standing and ongoing debates about the nature of the social sciences. These are characterised by methodological and disciplinary diversity." (NERF, 2000: 2).

The NERF Sub-group, like Tooley, embrace the diversity of methods which are employed in Education Studies, arguing that no effort should be made to restrict or constrain that diversity. Again, I shall argue, in contrast to this position, that it cannot be assumed that theoretical frameworks are available 'off the peg' in the various social sciences.

Education Studies brings together the key issues of social science theory in a particularly demanding way. Education, or at least teaching, is a vocation and consequently most people engaged in education have a positive interest in improving the conduct of education, learning and teaching. At the same time they recognise that the learning which an individual can achieve is crucially dependent upon the motivation, determination, effort and personal integrity of the learner. They also recognise that learning is influenced by the interaction in groups of peers, exchanges between learners and teachers, and by other circumstances in the learners' background. Good educational research needs to address the active learner as a knowing agent in their own development and also as a participant in social networks. These considerations place a minimum requirement upon educational researchers to use theoretical frameworks which are adequate for describing educational situations. In the first two chapters of this book I shall be teasing out the minimum criteria for what may be described as 'good theory'.

In the debate in the USA the report of the National Research Council is much more prescriptive when it comes to the issue of theory, describing one particular approach as 'more successful':

> "Turning to a line of work that we regard as scientifically more successful in a series of four randomised experiments Baumeister, Bratslavsky, Muraven and Tice (1998) tested three competing theories of 'will power' (or, more technically, 'self-regulation') – the psychological characteristic that is posited to be related to persistence with difficult tasks such as studying or working on homework assignments. One hypothesis was that will power is a developed skill that would remain roughly constant across repeated trials. The second theory posited a self-control schema 'that makes use of information

6

about how to alter one's own response' (p. 1254), so that once activated on one trial it would be expected to increase will-power on a second trial. The third theory, anticipated by Freud's notion of the ego exerting energy to control the id and superego, posits that will-power is a depletable resource - it requires the use of 'psychic energy' so that performance from trial 1 to trial 2 would decrease if a great deal of will-power was called for on trial 1. In one experiment, 67 introductory psychology students were randomly assigned to a condition in which either no food was present or both radishes and freshly baked chocolate chip cookies were present, and the participants were instructed either to eat two or three radishes (resisting the cookies) or two or three cookies (resisting the radishes). Immediately following this situation, all participants were asked to work on two puzzles that unbeknownst to them, were unsolvable, and their persistence (time) in working on the puzzles was measured. The experimental manipulation was checked for every individual participating by researchers observing their behaviour through a one-way window. The researchers found that puzzle persistence was the same in the control and cookie conditions and about 2.5 times as long, on average, as in the radish condition, lending support to the psychic energy theory – arguably, resisting the temptation to eat the cookies evidently had depleted the reserve of self-control, leading to poor performance on the second task." (Shavelson and Towne, 2002: 78)

At one level one can see why this approach is described as more successful. The three theoretical positions are outlined and a test which purports to be able to distinguish between those three positions is described and implemented. On the other hand none of the theoretical positions which are described can be said to take into account the active decision making of the participants or their ability to exercise free will; their relationship with researchers, their willingness to please the researchers and the impact upon their motivation of the various 'treatments' is completely ignored. The responses of the participants are assumed to be determined by the circumstances in which they are placed.

In many ways the research described is emblematic of much of the research which has been conducted in the area of Education Studies. The performance of the participants is seen as an effect of certain environmental causes, without the intervention of the conscious human agency of the participants themselves. In those terms we know a great deal about educational performance. We know that girls perform better than boys in school-leaving examinations at the age of 16 in the UK. And we know that children from middle class homes do better in school than do children from working class homes. As a description of what happens in education such research makes a good starting point.

However, when those same understandings are turned into explanations for educational processes we recognise their shortcomings. In the 1960s and 1970s the dangers of labelling children were recognised. Labelling children as slow learners, or likely to fail within the educational system, was regarded as reprehensible because the descriptions themselves could become part of the educational process. Labels influenced the teachers' expectations and therefore had an influence upon educational outcomes.

In the experiment reported above, as soon as we move beyond the interesting description of the differences between those who have been fed radishes and those who have been fed cookies and start looking at causal explanations, the weaknesses of theory in Education Studies becomes apparent. Once we start looking for mechanisms of how the differences come about, we see that the theoretical frameworks which have been put forward lose sight of individual participants, their feelings and their decisions. We have been presented with three theories of 'will-power', but those three theories actually leave no room for the exercise of individual choice and determination. Persistence is no longer a matter of will, but is caused by the presence or absence of chocolate chip cookies.

The other side of this theoretical coin has become prominent in the 1980s and 1990s where many participants in education have seen labelling of themselves as being liberating. Many people with dyslexia have argued that in calling themselves 'dyslexics' they feel relieved that their problem has been 'identified'. Their learning difficulties are externalised as a cause over which they have no control. They are content to have their free will circumscribed by such an understanding, because at the same stroke they are relieved of the responsibility for their own learning. Ironically, this act of labelling, or self-labelling, can now be seen as liberating. The theoretical understanding which we have developed, driven by a model of human behaviour which is caused by hereditary and environmental influences, removes freedom of choice at the same time as it relieves individuals of responsibility.

When we seek to develop educational theories to explain the operation of educational processes and to develop policies in education, we need to have criteria for successful theories. In general what we currently 'know' about education through educational research amounts to a range of generalised descriptions; we know who will do well in education, in a very general sense. When we wish to go beyond those descriptive accounts, we need to apply criteria which are much more demanding. In particular, we need to look for theories which can take into account, or at the very least leave room for, individual choice and individual responsibility.

With those reflections in mind it is possible to set out some basic minimum criteria which theory in Education Studies must meet. The first point is that education is essentially a human and ethical activity. Any attempt to theorise must be based upon sound ethical principles.

My starting point for dealing with ethical considerations is Kant's *Critique of Practical Reason*. Kant (1993) argues that in order to behave in an ethical way one must act in accordance with a principle. Moreover, for a principle to be ethical one must be capable of wishing that it should be universally applicable. I would extend this to argue that, theories in the area of Education Studies should be designed in such a way as to be universally applicable. For example, where a particular theory of learning is invoked, an effort should be made to apply it consistently to everybody involved in the study. In particular, I would argue that this means that theorists should be willing to see their theories applied to their own activities. Which educational researcher would be willing to see the fruits of years of their labour described as the natural outcome of a constellation of environmental and hereditary factors, for which they were not due any particular credit?

In my view, the idea that we should treat participants in educational research with due ethical consideration has been incorrectly interpreted to mean that only those people who are involved in an educational situation can theorise about that situation. This is an unnecessarily narrow interpretation of Kant's principle.

There is a particular difficulty for outside observers trying to theorise educational processes. As can be seen from the example from the National Research Council current educational theories which go beyond the descriptive tend to rely upon causal explanations. Causal explanations suggest a determinism in human behaviour which is unwarranted and removes both freedom of choice from the participants in a theoretical sense and also removes responsibility for their actions. One way out of this dilemma is to insist that it is illegitimate for an external observer to impose their understanding upon those who are being observed. But this is neither a necessary nor a sufficient condition for ensuring that the theory produced will be ethical. It is not sufficient because participant observers may themselves impose models which are causal and which undermine the free will and responsibility of those taking part. And it is not necessary because sensitive external observers who can frame theory which permits the accommodation of free will and responsibility can legitimately present their interpretations without overstepping the ethical boundaries.

The central point of applying Kant's ethical standard to educational theory is that it would prohibit the use of deterministic models which reduce the possibility of free will among participants and which remove responsibility for personal choices within educational settings. However, a number of consequences flow from this.

A causal, or mechanical, model of human behaviour suggests that a homogeneous group of individuals should always respond to a particular situation in the same way. We tend, in descriptive terms, to talk about the behaviour of groups within educational settings. Girls do better than boys in examinations or middle class children are more successful than working class children. However, effective theorising about the mechanisms at play in educational settings must not fall into the trap of, what I shall call, 'single-centredness'. Experience teaches us that within a group of children who are on all measurable variables similar, some will respond to their setting in a different way from other members of the same group. A teenager who plans their future in terms of being a football player or a pop star may not be very different in terms of their background and experiences from the teenager who plans to go to university and work towards a professional career. What differentiates these contrasting ambitions is an act of will on the part of the participant involved in education. Ethical educational theories must leave room for such diverse ambitions and actions of will.

The current educational imagination in educational theory suggests that those individuals who seek different outcomes must have been subject, at some earlier stage, to different influences. I would argue that this assumption is itself a denial of the free will which young people exercise as they make educational choices. Ethical educational theory must be complex enough to recognise the fact that similar individuals follow different paths through the educational system and seek and achieve different outcomes.

This 'multi-centredness' or variety of behaviour within homogeneous groups is not captured within current educational theory. Where apparently homogeneous groups have different outcomes, this is assumed to be attributable to 'error' in specifying the original causal models. In developing the kind of theory in Education Studies which will be useful as a basis for developing an understanding of educational systems and will be useful in developing approaches to policy making, we must look for models which are 'multi-centred' rather than 'single-centred'.

In developing theories which are single-centred, educational researchers frequently go one step further to stigmatise those responses which they cannot comprehend within their theoretical position, or to develop what I shall call a 'pathology of difference'. The teenager who plans their future as a football player or pop star may be ill advised. It may even be sensible to draw to their attention the relative probabilities of success in their chosen career. But this is very different from describing those choices in negative terms or bemoaning their 'drop out' from the educational system as dysfunctional. The educational theories which we seek must be capable of recognising that there are different routes through the maze of educational choices which young people have to make and that none is intrinsically more valuable than any other.

Finally, the allowance of free will and responsibility within educational theory means that there must be partial autonomy between the various different levels of educational systems. We must theorise educational systems so that the behaviour of individuals is not determined by the average performance of their social group, whether that is their school

12

peer group, their social class or their nation state. Clearly the life chances and educational opportunities of each individual will be partially shaped by those broader social influences, but only partly. Similarly the school ethos is not the precise sum of individual attitudes within the institution. We need theoretical frameworks which allow us to examine those links without assuming that there are deterministic and causal connections between the different levels of educational study.

To recap briefly, there is a debate about the quality of educational research both in the United Kingdom and in the USA. That debate highlights a number of shortcomings in the current educational literature, especially a failure of each generation of educational researchers to build upon what has gone before and a failure on the part of policy-makers to use the results of educational research in the development and improvement of policy. For the most part, those failures are attributed to individual shortcomings in the application of accepted methods and theories. The perceived lapses in quality in educational research are not seen as grounds for examining the fundamental theoretical frameworks which are used in Education Studies.

In contrast with this position I argue that the present symptoms identified in the debate about quality in educational research reflect a crisis in the kinds of theories which are being applied to educational settings. Current educational research does not provide a foundation for future development either by later researchers or by policy-makers, because the theories do not match up to certain minimum criteria.

I have suggested here, and will illustrate more fully later, a number of criteria which good educational theory should meet. Educational theory should:

- be ethical in allowing scope for individual free will
- be multi-centred in allowing that there is more than one correct way to develop one's educational career

- should allow for partial autonomy between levels of understanding; between the individual, the school and society more broadly.

The consequences of applying these criteria are far reaching, and will be examined in subsequent chapters. The proposed criteria implicitly provide a critique of much current educational research which is deterministic, single-centred and presupposes a strong linkage between the individual and the social group. Unless we can clear the ground and establish a framework which allows educational research to develop a cumulative tradition, we shall not make any progress towards the goals which are clearly set out within the debate on quality in educational research.

However, by setting the debate about the quality in educational research in terms of replicability and studies which develop upon previous research, and by insisting that educational theory has a place within the broader context of social *science*, the debate stresses certain features of educational theory. In particular it places a debate about the quality of educational research within a setting of theory in the sciences more generally. Therefore, before embarking upon detailed examples of how educational theory might be developed, I wish to take a slight detour in Chapter 2, to see what we can learn about the use of theory in the physical sciences and to see what of value might be learned in that process.

CHAPTER TWO: CLEARING THE GROUND

In this chapter I am going to build upon the criteria for good theory which I have set out in Chapter 1 and describe how these criteria can be met by borrowing from the physical sciences. The project of improving the social sciences by borrowing methods from the physical sciences was first set out by Auguste Comte (1999) and is normally described as positivism. In general, and for very good reasons, positivism has a bad name, because it is normally associated with transferring a very mechanical and causal understanding of the sciences to the social sciences.

Positivism normally involves transferring the latest understanding from the physical sciences to the social or human sciences. People are to be understood as pieces of sophisticated clockwork, as hydraulic systems or as the latest in computer software. Our group behaviour is to be described in terms of statistics designed to solve actuarial problems in the late nineteenth century. But in all cases, people are treated as objects of study rather than as human agents responsible for their own developments. I find the treatment of individuals as objects as offensive as anybody does, but the solution lies in the sensitive transfer of insights from the physical sciences, not in the outright rejection of all transfer.

The field of Education Studies is radically under-theorised. There is relatively little theory in the field of education, and even less consensus as to theory which is agreed. There are pressures which are directed towards keeping it so, both internal to the field and external. Among the external inhibitors of theory we can include government policy, while the internal pressures include a naïve adoption of the principles of action research and postmodernism. I shall return to these inhibitors of theoretical development later, but before I do so, I want to examine further the question of why theory in science retains such power, even though claims to it providing the truth must be rejected.

Paradoxically, the rejection of theory in Education Studies is coupled with a naïve recognition of the explanatory power of science, and the 'discoveries' of science are transferred into an understanding of Education Studies in a thoroughly disreputable and damaging way; e.g. 'scientists' have discovered a cure for Attention Deficit Hyperactivity Disorder (ADHD), or identified the gene responsible for ability in mathematics. The field has minimal theory of its own, but is awash with scientific notions which educationists are unable to evaluate or contextualise effectively.

Laws and Scientific Method

The starting point for finding a way forward has to be a recognition that when we look at 'laws' we have been focusing on entirely the wrong features. Theories and laws appear powerful because they are true. Our first concern has been to find true laws. When those laws turn out not to be true, we not unnaturally conclude that they are useless, and either turn to other laws which we believe to be true, or reject the notion of laws and theory altogether. But by focusing on the truth of laws, we are ignoring other important features which laws can have. So the first way to move forwards is to ask what other functions laws can have, besides embodying the truth.

One approach to this is to ask why we spend so much time teaching science which we know to be wrong in school. Why teach Newtonian physics when it has been replaced by relativity? A first attempt at this question, the most common answer, if you like, is that false laws can still be an approximation to the truth. Hooke's Law may not describe the behaviour of any actual spring, wire or elastic band, but it is a shorthand way of approximately recording the behaviour of all wires, springs and elastic bands. In fact, many springs may then actually be made to conform to Hooke's Law, so that the law works, but in that other sense of the word law, as an edict which sets out the way springs ought to behave.

This is a beguiling answer, and, of course, embodies much that is true. Boyle's Law and Charles's Law may not describe the behaviour of any gas, but they permit the description of a fictional 'ideal' gas, to which real gases approximate so long as they are a long way from liquefaction. But in providing this answer, we are still focusing upon truth as the ultimate test of a law. Denied the claim to truth, the law may still hang on to the vestige of legitimacy by laying claim to an approximate truth. This keeps us concentrated upon the content of the law as truth, and distracts us from what else the law could do.

The real strength of laws lies elsewhere. What laws do is to permit us to distinguish between that which needs an explanation, and that which does not need an explanation. Reduced to its simplest terms, Hooke's Law states that when we pull the ends of a spring, wire, thread or rubber band, it gets longer. This much seems obvious, hardly in need of an explanation.

Insofar as rubber bands, wires and springs all get longer as you pull harder on them, their behaviour needs no explanation. But rubber bands and copper wires do not follow Hooke's Law exactly. As a rubber band is extended it becomes harder to stretch, while copper wires become easier to stretch, as shown in Figure 2.1.

What needs explaining is why a rubber band becomes 'stronger' as it is extended, requiring progressively more force to produce each additional millimetre of extension, while a copper wire becomes progressively 'weaker' requiring less force to produce each successive millimetre of extension. Conformity with the law does not require explanation, while deviation from it does.

Figure 2.1: Hooke's Law

Hooke's Law states that the extension of a wire, spring etc. is proportional to the force applied. Or graphically, the graph representing applied force plotted against extension is a straight line.

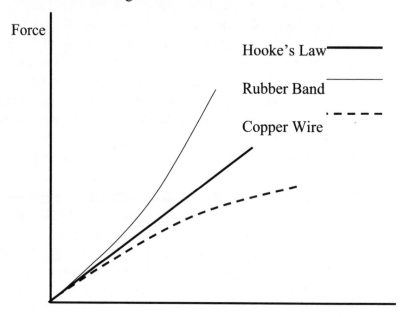

Kuhn (1962) has drawn attention to the existence of 'scientific revolutions', periods of scientific turmoil when one law or theory is rejected and discarded and another takes its place. In between revolutions there are periods of 'normal science', when scientists devote themselves to solving 'puzzles'. The term 'puzzle' is not supposed to indicate that normal science is a trivial occupation. Normal science concerns the application of theories to novel situations, and extending the range of application of theories. For example, after Newton had set out a framework for understanding the motion of bodies, there followed a long period in which those principles were applied to a wide range of physical situations, including sub-atomic particles.

Kuhn's study focuses upon revolutions, and relegates normal science to a secondary place. However, we can see that this perspective is produced by focusing, yet again, on the truth content of laws and theories. In periods of normal science, laws have an entirely different function; to highlight anomalies which need to be explained, or brought to order within the framework of theory.

Another example may help to clarify this function. Before Galileo it was thought that being stationary was natural; a force was required to explain why any body which was in motion moved. However, once Galileo had introduced the modern concept of inertia, the picture changed entirely. Galileo then knew that bodies on which there is no external force continue moving in a straight line forever. Steady motion in a straight line becomes 'natural' and what needs explaining is deviation from straight line motion. In order to explain now why planets travel in circles, a whole new machinery of gravitational forces is necessary. Nothing looks quite the same again when a new law or theory is adopted, because different phenomena are selected as the basis for puzzle solving. And in this theories are not equivalent since they produce different puzzles.

This function of laws in dividing phenomena into those which do not need explaining and those which do need explaining has been almost completely ignored (or in Kuhn's case relegated to a secondary role) because we have focused upon the truth value of laws and theories.

It should now be clear that what is intuitively obvious, or counts as 'common sense', is itself relative to the laws and theories which one holds to be true at any point. Once one has discarded the need for laws to be true, or even to offer approximations to the truth, one can take a more realistic stance on their role in defining that which is intuitively obvious. A theory can be taken up in order to examine those elements of phenomena which 'need explaining' in terms of that law. Later, that theory can be put aside, and another taken up, in order to examine those features which the first theory had assigned to the category of 'not in need of explanation'. The arbitrary nature of that which is obvious can be embraced along with the arbitrary nature of which theories are adopted. 'Common sense' is created by consensus, and does not have any prior, *a priori*, claim upon our attention.

It is in this sense that I would claim that an understanding of what theory is, and equally important, what it is not, should be transferred from the physical sciences to the human sciences, including Education Studies.

It may seem that I have now embraced a fully postmodern position of anything goes, in terms of theory, and it is important to explain why that is not the case, and why, although the choice of theory may be arbitrary, that is not at all the same as claiming that all theories are equally good. Positivism, in the sense of transferring the methodology of the physical sciences to the human sciences, has been rightly criticised for treating human, moral agents as inert objects of study. This is a criticism which needs to be taken seriously, and points in some very specific directions for future study in Education Studies. The major disservice which postmodernism inflicts upon the human sciences is that it reduces the role of theory to nothing. Theory is poorly articulated, and as a consequence educational research is driven along on the basis of conflicting, half-understood, and amoral prejudices which can never be examined.

Let me stress this point. The decision that some things need explaining rather than others implies a theoretical position. But the adoption of clear theoretical positions is rendered illegitimate within a postmodern framework which assumes that, because no true theories have been found, all theory can be discarded. The consequence is that implicit theoretical positions are adopted which are not readily available for critique or development. Such a position is deeply destructive of the development of improved understandings, and leaves only violence or the market place to decide issues which should be available for intellectual examination. It also undermines any attempt to build upon previous work and develop frameworks which will facilitate the improvement of policy.

The insight which we should be transferring from the physical sciences to the human sciences is captured by Albert Einstein in a characteristically pithy aphorism: "It is the theory that decides what we can observe"(Heisenberg, 1969: 79-80). But the converse is also true; if we claim to be observing anything, it is because we are applying theory, although frequently that theory will be implicit, under-developed, and masquerading as common sense. We should be particularly sceptical of those who claim to know what 'reality' is, especially when they disavow an interest in theory, or critique theory in terms of its failure to engage with 'reality'. This is little more than a rhetorical device to protect their own theoretical position by hiding that theory from examination.

Through the 1960s Comparative Education, like many other fields within Education Studies, was divided on methodological grounds. The field was defined, if it was defined by anything, by debates about how studies should be conducted. From the 1980s onwards, such debates were largely put to one side with the argument that we should get on with conducting studies, rather than debating methodology. The result has been a proliferation of case studies, but a failure to establish the means whereby studies could contribute to an accumulation of knowledge (as commented upon by Tooley (1998) and others). The importance of those methodological debates, which remain unresolved, has not been fully acknowledged. Comparative Education is a fertile area for examining the implicit assumptions which individuals, groups and governments hold in relation to Education Studies. By focusing upon that which is socially constructed, it highlights the shortcomings of universalising assumptions.

Currently, with the mapping of the human genome, we are frequently exposed to the most generalising of all scientific approaches to the human condition, the science of genetics. We are used to receiving sweeping claims in the press, or broadcast news, that scientists have isolated the gene which determines this or that. For example, the genes which dispose one towards homosexuality, left-handedness or dyslexia have been identified. By extension, we have become used to the idea that one is born homosexual, left-handed or dyslexic. Comparative Education, however, disposes one to ask difficult questions, and provides the material to explore the social construction of these phenomena. What does the distinction between left- and right-handedness mean in Hindu society where the different, socially acceptable functions of the left and right hand are clearly defined for all members of society? How does dyslexia exhibit itself in an ideographic culture such as China or Japan?

To see how pervasive these 'scientific' assumptions (and their implicit theoretical positions) have become, consider the fact that we now routinely speak of a person as being 'gay' or 'straight'. We forget that in some societies sexuality is constructed, not as a permanent state, but as a series of stages through which a person proceeds. I am reminded of the saying I heard when I was in the Middle East thirty years ago: "For children, a woman; for pleasure a boy; but for sheer ecstasy a ripe watermelon". This dictum suggests to me that sexuality is not something which is an expression of genetic determination.

Apparently, scientists working on the genome project were surprised that there were so few genes in the human genome. They should not have been so surprised. There are not enough genes to account for all the traits for which we are in the habit of expecting genetic answers. A student of Comparative Education would hardly be surprised at this discovery.

The other, and equally pernicious, set of assumptions which we find in Education Studies relates to socialisation. Girls are socialised into being passive and having lower career expectations, and end up in menial jobs. Boys are socialised into believing in their own abilities, being ambitious and seeking high status careers such as medicine. Working class children are socialised to need instant gratification of their needs and wants, while middle class children are socialised to defer gratification and take the long term view. In both cases, what can we learn from the USSR, where women doctors outnumbered their male colleagues and social class was constructed very differently? Socialisation is itself, of course, socially constructed, and should be the subject of critical examination in cross-cultural contexts. Yet attempts at such cross-cultural studies (for example the IEA studies of academic achievement) have been singularly unsuccessful in accounting for differences.

In this, as in so much else, the Soviet Union was a major challenge to implicit theoretical assumptions, and I have long thought that from a Comparative Education perspective, if the USSR had not existed it would have been necessary to invent it.

The problem with both the genetic approach and the socialisation approach (the nature or the nurture) is that both start from the assumption that the right way of understanding education systems is through the individual. Social groups are aggregates of individuals, and if one understood the genetic make-up or socialisation patterns of all individuals in the system, then we would be able to understand the system as a whole. This is the normal way in which the physical sciences proceed, and it is the last poor lesson from the physical sciences which we need to reject.

Where does that leave us in terms of a positive direction in which we can go in the field of Education Studies? There are three lessons which we should learn from these considerations. The first lesson is that, in spite of everything postmodernists and others have said, there remains a need for theory. Even accepting that theory is arbitrary, we should pick up the most developed and explicit theory and use it to define the scope of particular studies. We might, for example, take up an economic theory, that people act so as to maximise their individual returns. This serves a function of defining that which needs explaining and that which does not need explaining. In the case of this example, when people *do* act to maximise their economic returns, that does *not* need explaining. When they act in a way which does *not* maximise their individual returns, that *does* need explaining. That (economic) assumption can be put aside and examined at a later date, but theories should be used to define rigorous studies which can develop our understanding of educational processes.

The second lesson, which comes from the critique of the sciences rather than from the sciences themselves, is that there is a moral imperative to treat all people as active and intelligent agents rather than as objects of study. To draw from Kant again, I would say that this should take the form of a universal principle, that a law which can be applied to any group of people should be equally capable of being applied to all people, including the person proposing the law.

Let me examine this a little further. I am subject to the laws of physics. The Law of Gravity states that I will be pulled towards the ground, and the Second Law of Thermodynamics states that order in the Universe will tend to decrease. But that does not mean that I lie flat on the floor while my body decays. Eventually I will and it will, but in the meantime, I obey the laws of physics while struggling against their consequences.

It does not make sense for me to think about genetic determination or socialisation in those terms. They are an affront to my personal agency in the sense that they suggest my struggling against them is meaningless. They deny me free will. If on the other hand, I admit free will, then my agency denies the efficacy of the laws as explanations. (Note that it makes perfectly good sense to say that, overall and in the long run, people tend to act so as to maximise their economic returns, but at this moment I am going to act otherwise for some other, probably moral, purpose.)

This brings me to the third and most radical conclusion about theory in Education Studies, not about what it should do and should be, but about what it should not do and should not be. It should not aim to build up an understanding of groups from an understanding of the individuals who compose those groups. It should, in fact, say nothing about individuals.

Game Theory Models

It may be difficult to visualise what a theory of Education which says nothing about individuals would look like, so let me give an example from game theory, specifically a two person non-zero sum game or co-operative game. Non-zero sum games are games where there is an element of competition and there is also an element of co-operation where the pay-off for the players may not be zero in total. The non-zero sum game takes several different forms depending on the exact nature of the pay-off matrix. One of the forms is the game of 'Chicken'. 'Chicken' is a very simple game in which two players drive cars towards each other in opposite directions, and the object of the exercise is to avoid deviating from the straight line that they are driving along. Obviously, if neither of them turn off the straight line they collide in an accident which is disastrous for both of them. If one of them turns off, the one who does not turn off, wins. But they both derive some benefit in the sense that they have not been involved in a disastrous accident. However, the one who has not turned off is deemed the winner and is therefore better off than the one who has turned off. This can be drawn up in a pay-off matrix shown below. What does this understanding of non-zero sum games tell us? And can it have an application in a social setting?

Figure 2.2: A pay-off matrix for the game of Chicken

		Player A	
		Drive Straight	Swerve off Central Line
Player B	Swerve off Central Line	5 / -5	0 / 0
	Drive Straight	-10 / -10	-5 / 5

[Value of game to A shown in upper right section of each square; value of game to B in lower left.]

Many years ago, when I was a teacher in secondary school, I had a class in which there was a pair of twin brothers. I became extremely interested in the issue of twins, not least because I noticed that the vast majority of my colleagues did not bother to differentiate between the two twin brothers.

A consequence of the fact that the teachers did not differentiate between them was that they received praise or blame equally, irrespective of the contribution which either had made to a particular piece of work. That is to say, they could both produce a piece of work and they would both be given equal praise or equal blame for good or bad work. Faced with that situation, they had a range of possible courses of action available to them. They could both have worked hard to produce good work and they would then be equally praised, or they could both be idle and produce poor work and receive equal blame for the shortcomings of their work. But there was another solution, which was that one of them could work hard and produce good work, and the other, with minimum effort, could copy it from him and they would receive equal praise or blame for the quality of the work.

Figure 2.3: Pay-off matrix for Twins

		Twin A	
		Do nothing/ copy B's work	Work hard
Twin B	Work Hard	5 / -5	0 / 0
	Do nothing/ Copy A's work	-10 / -10	-5 / 5

One can relatively easily see that the game in which they were involved had a very similar structure to 'Chicken'. There they both were, sitting at their desk in the classroom, doing nothing, driving head on towards the wreck. If neither of them did anything, then they would eventually arrive, both of them with poor work, in a situation where they received high levels of blame for poor work. But if one of them decided to work, the second, his brother, could copy the work from him. They would both receive benefits from this course of action. But the one who had been obliged to do the work would have to invest more effort and therefore was slightly worse off than the one who copied.

Over a period of time, I decided to devote some study to the question of identical twins and I learned, among other things, that identical twins are not always strictly identical. They are very frequently the mirror image of each other. Armed with this piece of information, I went back to my classroom and looked at the twins in my class with greater care and noticed that they were, indeed, not identical but mirror images of each other in physical terms. One parted his hair on the left, the other parted his hair on the right and so on. As soon as I had learned how to distinguish accurately, they were no longer involved in a game of 'Chicken' because each of them would be praised or blamed in accordance with the effort which I saw them making. But it continued to be the case that very many of my colleagues did not distinguish between them and I could see that in very many situations it was to their benefit that one of them worked and the other one did not.

What we can see in the logic of the situation in which identical twins find themselves is that there is very strong pressure towards differentiation. Two individuals with identical genetic inheritance and in identical environmental settings actually have a very strong incentive to respond completely differently to that situation. Literature abounds with examples of twins who are strongly different to the extent of one being good and the other being evil. But a scientific imagination and particularly our present day scientific imagination does not embrace that concept. We take from the physical sciences of biology and genetics an intuition which says that genetically identical twins will be expected to behave in identical ways within a similar environmental setting. And in popular imagination this is shown in films such as *The Boys from Brazil* where an attempt is made to clone an individual. The whole precept of the film is that with identical genetic material and with controlled, similar environmental backgrounds the outcome will be similar in every case.

In fact, looking at the situation of twins as a non-zero sum game leads us to the exact opposite intuition; a twin is a person who is faced with the existence of somebody who is physically identical. There is a very strong logic to the situation which dictates that those twins would seek to establish their own personal identity as different from their twin's. And that casts a very interesting light on a number of issues which are to be found within educational research. In studies of identical twins, the evidence suggests that twins perform better, on average, if they are separated, treated differently and dressed differently, so that people can relatively easily differentiate between them. But it also has some implications for a number of practices in education, such as the use of the school uniform, where we appear artificially to be reducing differences between the individuals we have in front of us as teachers.

It is also worth noting what the game theory model does not tell us. It does not tell us which of the two twins is going to work hard and which of them is going to copy. Nor does it even say that one of the twins will always be the one who works hard and the other will always be the one who copies. There is plenty of scope here for differentiation. For example, one twin may become interested in languages, the other twin in sciences or mathematics. What the model does say is that differentiation is likely but everything else which pertains to the free will, the choice, the volition, the likes and dislikes of individual twins is not addressed by the game theory model. There is, as it were, a hole at the centre of the model which leaves space for free will, decision and, incidentally, for praise or blame on the basis of performance.

The gap at the middle of game theory models is precisely the gap which is consistent with Kant's categorical imperative. The categorical imperative requires that people be treated as ends and not as means, and consequently that their free will and moral responsibility for their decisions should be recognised. The model says that it is likely, but no stronger than likely, that two twins will differentiate themselves, one working hard, the other not working hard. But the model does not say that working hard is determined in the case of one and that not working hard is determined in the case of the other. The model places no restriction or develops no understanding which is in conflict with the notion of free will.

It is true to say that the game theory model is one which I, as an observer, have imposed upon the two twins that I am looking at. This is not their analysis of the world. It is not necessarily how they perceive their activity but it is an external understanding imposed upon them. In that sense, it meets the requirement of looking like a model from the physical sciences which has been developed for social understanding. But even though it is not their own analysis, because it does not contradict their human agency it does seem to me to be the kind of model which would be compatible with Kant's categorical imperative.

I cannot answer, of course, for everybody else but it seems to me that this kind of analysis is one which I would find acceptable if applied to me.

Again, it is worth stressing how different this analysis is from current understanding which we have in our everyday imagination of education. What we are looking at here is a quite different imagination, a different way of thinking about individuals in social action.

Recently I was sitting in a meeting with two colleagues, one of whom was describing what I think we would all regard as a model student - intelligent, diligent, full of insight and reflection on their own performance as a student. The other colleague remarked that she wished that such students could be cloned. Although this was clearly said in jest, it does illustrate the extent to which the genetic model has so gripped our imagination that in those few words one can express the insight that a good student is determined in their performance by the simple inheritance of genetic material.

There is a further and perhaps more important lesson to be drawn from this simple comment. It is that the failure to develop theoretical models in education and the social sciences does not mean that we take an atheoretical approach to education or the social sciences. What appears to happen is that the absence of good theory in our field of study means that we draw upon rather inferior models from the physical sciences and biological sciences. A failure to develop theory in education does not result in a lack of theory in education; on the contrary, it promotes precisely that naïve transfer of understanding from the physical sciences which we sought to avoid in the first place. This is not exactly the methodological equivalent of Gresham's Law that the bad money drives out good. It is not that bad theory drives out good theory but it certainly appears to be the case that in the absence of good theory, bad theory rushes in to fill the gap. A determination not to produce bad theory results in a reliance upon relatively poor theory, whether taken in a naïve way from psychology or sociology or directly from the physical and biological sciences.

I have presented the case of identical twins as an example of theory which is useful in describing a complex situation. It conforms to the criteria which I have set out in Chapter 1. It takes as intuitively obvious that people act so as to increase their own benefit, although they may define this differently from other actors in their environment. It draws attention to certain features which are not in need of explanation, but highlights other areas of action which are in need of explanation. In addition, it sets out an understanding which does not contain specific restrictions on the way any individual will act, but rather concentrates upon the emergent properties of a system – the way the collective operates is detached from the psychological responses of the individuals who make up the system.

The game theory model does not prescribe how each of the twins should behave in every situation; it simply suggests that we would normally expect one of them to be doing most of the work in any particular lesson. It allows scope for each of the twins to exercise free will, and to develop his own tastes, and in doing so, permits them to be held responsible for their own contribution to the work. In that way, it meets my first criterion of being ethical and allowing scope for individual free will.

The game theory model is multi-centred as it admits multiple ways in which the tastes and talents of the two twins can be combined. Moreover, in any particular environment, it suggests that not working might be a perfectly rational response on the part of one of the twins. We can begin to understand what positive benefit he derives. We are less tempted to think that he is pathologically lazy or suffers from some deficiency. In this way the game theory model meets my second criterion of being multi-centred.

And finally the game theory model allows for partial autonomy between levels of understanding. It explains why we would expect a (collective) pattern of behaviour where one twin works and the other does not, but it says nothing about the individual behaviour of either twin in isolation. In this way it meets my third criterion for good theory.

To suggest that theory should say nothing about individuals, as I have done here, is to overstate the case for the sake of effect. There are, of course, legitimate areas of educational theory which deal with individuals; we know a great deal about how people learn, even if it is only the dictum of Carl Rogers: "We cannot teach another person directly; we can only facilitate his (sic) learning." (Barrett-Lennard,1998: 184) What is not overstating the case is that the knowledge of the individual cannot inform the system level understanding. Systems have emergent properties which cannot be arrived at through the summation of the parts.

Multi-person game theory offers an important model for how theory in Education Studies should be developed. It provides a macro-level explanation of a group phenomenon. (In this case, it explains why twins may behave very differently in spite of similarities in genetic inheritance and environment.) But it says absolutely nothing about which individuals will be involved. And by saying nothing about the individual, it leaves each individual with moral responsibility for their own actions. "Tough on crime, tough on the causes of crime", is actually a very difficult approach to theorise, unless one can achieve this division between the description of group behaviour and that of individual behaviour.

In later chapters in this book, I have tried to develop approaches to theory in Education Studies which attempt to draw upon the insights and methods of the physical sciences, without deteriorating into determinism at the individual level. I have looked at the use of linear programming in describing institutional planning, at two person game theory in studying career choices in education, at multi-person game theory, as in the case above, at voting theory in describing processes of policy adoption in institutions, and at chaos theory as a way of understanding managerial processes in large organisations. It is not, from my perspective, an accident that these various approaches are based on theories which have very strong mathematical affinities. To those who have taken less of an interest in mathematics than I have, they may appear to be an accidental (or, hopefully, fortuitous) collection of methods. However, in the subsequent exploration of these different approaches to theory in Education Studies, some of the similarities in the underlying mathematics will become clear.

One of the persistent problems which faces educationists is the description, or explanation, of situations where choices are made by participants in the educational process. Young people, for example, choose to leave schooling at the end of compulsory education or to stay on in further or higher education. And, by and large, young people do both of these things; some stay on in education and others leave.

If we take a simplistic view of what scientific theory can do, we will follow a route taken by many studies in education, and look for the 'causes' of such educational behaviour. We might, for example, look at the rate of return analysis of years spent in education, and conclude, as economists of education generally have, that education is one of the best investments which young people can make. This 'explains' why people stay on in education. It cannot, of course, explain what causes some people to leave.

Studies of a different kind will show that some people have been socialised into attitudes to education which 'cause' them to leave. Young women or working class youths are more susceptible to such influences, or find it harder to obtain accurate information to form a view of their own possible rate of return on investment in education, and consequently are predisposed to leaving. The fact remains that substantial numbers of women and the working class remain in education beyond the compulsory leaving age, but a causal approach cannot explain their behaviour. Some alternative cause is sought – role models among the teachers, an aspiring mother, or whatever takes the fancy of the researcher.

I shall return to the possibility of more complex models drawn from the physical sciences later (Chapters 7,8,9 and 10). But first I shall review current mainstream theories in the area of Education Studies, and the criticisms which have been offered of them. The review of these theories, together with their critiques, will show that the need for models which meet the criteria set at the end of Chapter 1 is generally recognised.

CHAPTER THREE: LARGE SCALE STATISTICAL SURVEY METHODS

Large scale survey methods are a development of scientific methods, based upon a nineteenth century view of science. The statistical methods employed have been refined, and are subject to continual refinement, but the underlying rationale of the methods is based upon J. S. Mill's theory of scientific method. Mill (1970) set out in perfectly logical detail the methods which could be used in the social sciences, based upon his understanding of the scientific method as practised in his time. Mill described three techniques which could be used in the development of an inductive social science. The first method was the method of similarities, the second the method of differences and the third a combination method of similarities and differences.

Statistical Methods

In the method of similarities what the investigator was supposed to look for were similarities in circumstances which produced the same effect. This is essentially a way of looking at causal relationships. Mill argued that if a phenomenon had a cause, then that cause would be present in every case where the effect was observed. Thus, for example if we take a poor educational performance to be an outcome and we are looking for the cause of that outcome, then we should look for those things which are invariably associated to poor educational performance. In that way, we would hope to identify the causes of the educational outcome which we sought to explain.

In the method of differences we would look at situations where there were different outcomes, some of which produced poor educational outcomes some of which did not. We would then look for the differences between those cases in order to identify those causes which were present when the outcome to be explained was present, and which were absent when the outcome was absent.

The method of similarities and differences is not a logically different method but involves looking at a range of situations which are both similar and different in the configuration of causes which are present and the configuration of outcomes.

Mill's account of the scientific method embodies three features which I have criticised strongly: his approach to scientific method focuses directly upon the importance of finding the truth; it focuses upon the identification of causes of particular outcomes; and it focuses upon what I have described as 'single-centredness'. Mill's method is directed to finding a homogenous group of causes which produce a reliable outcome.

In treating the important elements of human behaviour as causal, Mill's approach reduces human agents to mere ciphers who are not able to direct their own actions, but who respond to the circumstances in which they find themselves without the ability to exercise will-power. This is a dehumanising approach and undermines the moral insight which one can gain from studying human behaviour. Coupled with a foundation on a claim of discovering some objective truth, this position is criticised by those who think that moral aspects of the study of education are of overriding importance. This criticism finds expression, for example, in Habermas' (1984) notion of dialogue as the basis for the study of human action.

The single-centredness gives the scientific observer the ability to make sweeping generalisations about all sorts of human experience thereby removing 'colour' from that experience. It might be noted, however, that this same criticism was made of Newton by Blake who suggested that by generalising about mathematical abstractions, namely, bodies, Newton overlooked the richness and beauty of nature. Blake graphically represents this in his picture of Newton when Newton is studying abstract triangles which he is drawing on a piece of paper while the beauty and richness of nature goes on around him unobserved.

From an action research perspective McNiff (1992) criticises a scientific approach to education in very similar terms. She argues that, by making a spurious claim to objectivity, social science approaches to education miss the richness and subjectivity of individuals' experiences within educational settings.

Figure 3.1: William Blake's portrait of Newton

Mill's basic approach has been further developed in the statistical methods of regression, where numerical variation of the dependent variable is 'explained' in terms of the independent variables. Gilbert Peaker, who did much of the statistical work on the studies for the Plowden Report (1967) and for the early IEA studies, describes the method in terms of an analogy of handicapping a yacht race (Peaker, 1971). Suppose that we observe a yacht race which includes many different types of vessel. Those various yachts will have different maximum speeds depending on a number of design features. In particular, we will observe that longer boats tend to go faster than shorter boats. We could therefore handicap a yacht race in terms of the length of the boat. The observed times would be corrected in terms of a factor which depended upon the length of the boat. So, supposing that in raw times we observed a certain distribution among the boats, we could then apply a correction to the times to get a handicap time based upon the length of the boat; the spread of handicap times should be smaller than the spread of raw times. This can be illustrated in the diagram below. In Peaker's terms we would say that we have explained a certain amount of the difference in the performance of the boats in terms of the first independent variable, the length of the boats.

Figure 3.2: Handicapping Yacht Race Times

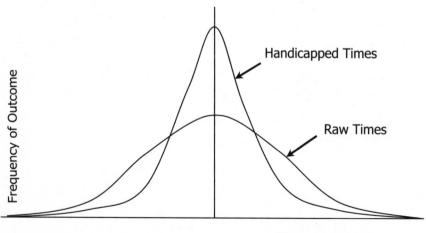

We can go on to add a second handicapping correction where we apply a correction, for example for the height of the mast, to the handicap times which have already been calculated. Again, because by and large yachts with tall masts go faster than yachts with short masts, we would produce a narrowing of the spread in the handicap times when compared with the handicapping which involved the length of the boat alone. In Peaker's terms we would have explained more of the variation in speed of boats by including two variables rather than one.

A third, fourth and a fifth variable can be added until we were satisfied that we had produced a satisfactory handicapping. For example, a third variable might be added such as the width of the boat. Again boats which are wider in the beam tend to go faster than boats which are narrow in the beam.

As Peaker describes it, the outcome of perfect handicapping is that all of the variation in time should have been removed and that the handicap times of all yachts should be exactly the same. In this way the ultimate goal of explaining all variation would have been achieved. However, in practice such perfect handicapping serves as an ideal rather than as a practical possibility.

In the IEA studies (Comber and Keeves, 1973: Martin, 2000; Mullis, 2000; Travers and Westburg, 1989; Robitaille and Garden, 1989; Burstein, 1992), Peaker's method was applied to maths scores. An attempt was made to explain variation in mathematics performance by including a wide range of 'handicapping' variables. Family background variables, such as the size of family, social position of parents and the education of parents were included, along with school variables relating to the size of classes and the qualifications of teachers.

In practice this handicapping produces extremely poor results, with as little as ten per cent of the variation being explained by the method. The goal of perfect handicapping – of explaining all of the causes which produce particular performance in particular tests – remains as an ideal towards which the method attempts to approach. The variation which is left unexplained at any particular point at which the study stops is referred to as 'error', indicating quite clearly that there is a desire to remove this random element of variation if at all possible.

These methods are clearly inductive and the philosophical foundations of inductive reasoning have been criticised by others, most obviously by Hume and by Popper. But there are other problems with these statistical methods.

The ultimate goal of regression analysis is to explain all of the variation in the dependent variables. If we suppose that such a study was pursued to a perfect conclusion, then all of the variation would have been explained. There would be no place for personal choice or effort in the generation of the dependent variable. Everything would be explained in terms of background causes. This is an example of what Archer (1995) describes as upward conflation; it removes the possibility that human agents play an active part in the development of their own performance in educational tests. For example, an individual's score in a maths test would be completely determined by their social setting. Such a theoretical conclusion, as I have set out elsewhere, is a contravention of Kant's prescription that we should only apply theory to individuals which treats them as active human agents.

There is a further difficulty with the method as Peaker describes it. In education, as in yachting, the independent variables are very strongly correlated. So long boats tend to have tall masts and be broad in the beam whereas short boats tend to have shorter masts and be narrower in the beam. In the same way in social circumstances the level of the education of parents tends to correlate with family size, with better income and with attendance at schools where teachers are better qualified. When the independent variables are so strongly correlated in this way, the association of any variation in the dependent variable with any specific independent variable is very difficult indeed, if not impossible. The identification of causes is arbitrary and related to the order in which we put the independent variables into the regression.

Peaker addresses this question quite directly in a specific case. In education, if one looks at the independent variables which alone account for most variation in the dependent variable, then teacher qualifications tend to figure very highly. Those children who attend schools where the teachers are well qualified and professionally active tend to do better than those children whose teachers are less active professionally and less well qualified. We might therefore argue that this makes teacher qualification and professional engagement an extremely important variable which can account for much of variation in pupil performance. However, Peaker argues that this line of reasoning would be muddle-headed because what is actually happening is that children who perform better in their early years of schooling tend to be selected to attend schools and classes where teachers are better qualified. He develops this line of argument into a rationale for the order in which one puts independent variables into the regression process. Since early events can affect later ones but later ones cannot affect earlier ones, variables which represent early childhood experience should go into the regression first. Home background variables and early schooling variables should be fed into the regression before teacher qualifications in the current life cycle of the child in school. The result is to leave a very small amount of the variation to be explained by teacher qualification.

A similar kind of problem can be seen arising in debates about the effect of class size upon educational performance. The broad picture which emerges from statistical studies is that children perform better in large classes than they do in small classes and this is sometimes completely erroneously taken to imply that there is an optimum size for classes somewhere between thirty and forty. However, simple regression analysis is rendered absolutely ineffective by the fact that children who are under-performing in schools tend to be selected to be put in special small groups or to be taught in classes with additional teacher support and adult support. The poor performance of a pupil will therefore bring about a smaller class size and this means that any overall statistic which tries to explain performance in school by class size is contaminated by an activity which is intended to improve the performance of under-achieving children.

Much of the debate around whether school performance is more affected by genetic inheritance or by social environment is similarly flawed by the fact that this method of regression analysis does not enable one to identify the contribution of specific causes to the performance of pupils.

Statistical methods have been considerably developed since Peaker's time and there are now highly complex models of regression which take into account school effects, class effects, family effects, and broader social effects. Attempts have been made to distinguish between those elements and strands in producing particular levels of pupil performance. However, the fact remains that regression analysis focuses upon identifying causes for specific outcomes and in focusing upon causes seeks to explain the variation between pupils. At the back of such a description of social events is the idea that, all other things being equal, every pupil would perform equally well in a maths test. One of the ironies of this is that the less variation there is in the dependent variable the harder it becomes to use the method. Peaker, for example, tries to explain his disappointment at how little schooling variables appear to affect outcomes in test scores. He explains his disappointment by the fact that schools, being fairly tightly regulated by governments, tend to show relatively less variation than families, which are less rigidly controlled by law and policy. It follows in terms of the method that family background is much more likely to be able to explain variation in school performance simply because there is more variation in family background variables than there is in school background variables.

The focus in regression analysis is always upon a basic assumption that given identical conditions the performance would be the same. I describe this as being a focus upon a single centre, or single-centredness. Such an approach can be contrasted with the models which I have set out in this book drawn from game theory. Game theory models do not include the assumption that in identical circumstances ostensibly equal individuals will behave in exactly the same way. This can be seen from studying the notion of the mixed strategy. Game theory assumes that individuals will distribute themselves across a number of outcomes rather than having a tendency towards focus upon a single outcome. Although the outcomes of regression analyses are always expressed in probabilistic or stochastic terms, these are not probabilities about distributions between outcomes but only probabilities which express our confidence that individuals come close to the single centre.

Michael Bassey (2001) has attempted to escape from this by introducing the notion of fuzzy generalisations. These might be expressed in terms such as children who have these particular background variables are likely to have mathematics test scores that fall between 50 per cent and 60 per cent. This leaves the possibility open that future analyses and improved data will allow us to narrow the range of generalisation so that that group of pupils identified by a particular range of independent variables will have maths test scores that range between 53 per cent and 57 per cent. Within his notion of fuzzy generalisations, Bassey retains the idea of a central tendency towards which our knowledge brings us. The ultimate goal would still be the prediction, with absolute certainty, of pupils' performance in schools.

At the end of Chapter 1 I set out three criteria which theory in Education Studies should meet. It should be ethical in allowing scope for individual free will. It should be multi-centred in allowing that individuals might choose different routes through the educational system. And it should allow for partial autonomy between levels of understanding; it should not be assumed that societal variables could account for individual outcomes. It will be clear that the statistical methods used in large scale quantitative research fail to meet all three criteria. Moreover, as has been noted, the statistical methods are ill suited to the task of deciding which cause is most influential in producing an outcome.

Notwithstanding these shortcomings, statistical survey methods have been extremely influential in shaping our common sense understanding of processes which are involved in schooling. Very many of the taken-for-granted assumptions about education, the things that we 'know' about how people learn, are popular generalisations from the results of statistical surveys. Some examples have already been mentioned, such as the effect of social class, the influence of genetic and environmental factors, the effect of class size, and so on. In fact, if we compiled a simple summary of what we currently know about education, most of the results would draw upon regression approaches and most of the results would be flawed for exactly the reasons which have been set out here. Working class children tend to do worse in school than middle class children. Children in large classes tend to perform better than children in small classes. Girls tend to perform less well in maths scores than boys do, although current evidence suggests that the opposite is now true and perhaps common sense would now tell us that girls perform better in maths tests than boys do.

Statistical survey methods, drawing upon the philosophical bases of Mill and Peaker, may provide a good starting point for theoretical investigation. They can produce descriptive generalisations as to what is generally the case. However, the attempt to move beyond the descriptive and into the identification of causes is invariably a mistake. The statistical methods are actually poorly equipped to provide an answer to the question of what causes good school performance or what causes poor school performance.

To develop theory which can help our understanding of how events come about in schools, and to provide a sound basis for future research or for the development of policy, we need explicit model building and testing.

One of the ironies of what I have described as single-centredness in educational theory is that variation is rarely that which needs explaining in educational terms. If a teacher went into a classroom and set a test and every pupil scored 55 per cent on the test, then the teacher would be looking for an explanation of the sameness, not for an explanation of variation. In real life, any practitioner would be deeply suspicious of a result in which every pupil scored exactly the same. In Peaker's terms, however, there would be nothing to explain.

From Description to Policy

One of the leading exponents of large-scale statistical survey methods of the kind pioneered by Peaker is Peter Mortimore. Mortimore has contributed extensively to such survey methods by developing improved techniques of looking at multi-level analysis to separate out the effects of schools, departments within schools, classes within schools, or other social background variables. He has also been involved in most of the major large-scale studies in the United Kingdom since Rutter's *Fifteen Thousand Hours*. In 1998 he published a book which reviewed his various contributions to statistical survey methods over the past thirty years. (Mortimore: 1998).

In spite of developments in the methods which Mortimore advanced, there remains the difficulty that such survey methods are single-centred. It is usual, indeed, one might almost say it is traditional, when authors set out the mechanics of survey methods that they include a couple of important disclaimers. The first disclaimer is that large-scale survey methods deal only with the averages or tendencies on a large-scale. For example Mortimore (1998: 168) states that,

> "It must be noted, however, that this definition does not assume that all students from disadvantaged backgrounds are likely to do badly in tests or examinations. Some of these individual students will do very well; they will buck the trend. What the

definition implies is that, all other things being equal, disadvantaged students as a group are less likely to do well than are those from advantaged backgrounds, in any kind of competitive assessment."

The second disclaimer, which it is usual to add, is that correlations do not give any indication of cause or relationships. However, in spite of these two disclaimers, the fact remains that correlation studies are deeply rooted in the notion that they are aiming to discover causal relationships, and that it is possible in general to identify similar outcomes for groups who are similar on input variables. This single-centredness for example is highlighted by Mortimore where group differences are compared (Mortimore, 1998: 188). This table makes it clear that girls can be expected to gain 4.1 GCSE points more than boys. That those who have no free school meals can be expected to score 5.2 GCSE points on average more than those with free school meals, and that on average each year of age adds 0.2 to the GCSE point score of the pupil. Such comparisons make it absolutely clear that we are looking at a concentration upon single-centredness.

In view of the fact that Mortimore stands at the very centre of the development of large-scale statistical survey methods, many of his comments upon the development of those methods are extremely illuminating. Not least his insistence upon developing multi-level approaches to statistical methods suggests that he has a concern for distinguishing between different levels, and for accommodating that partial autonomy between levels which I have drawn attention to as being so important. In a number of other ways, however, his evaluation of survey methods points to similar concerns about theoretical developments to those which I have voiced here.

Perhaps, over-arching all of Mortimore's discussion of survey methods, is an underlying difficulty at getting from 'school effectiveness' to 'school improvement'. He describes his early work as being firmly within the tradition of 'school effectiveness'. So his work on *Fifteen Thousand Hours* and *School Matters* is directed towards finding those correlations between school performance or school effectiveness, and corresponding patterns of organisation. In following this approach he provides a detailed description of schools as they are observed. But knowing what happens cannot give a clear direction of what ought to be done, and logically Mortimore is left with the difficulty that knowing a great deal about school effectiveness does not actually provide very much help or direction in developing plans and policies for school improvement.

As Mortimore expresses it (1998: 142),

> "This issue, which I have termed pivotal, leads away from studies of school effectiveness to the area of school improvement. The next two issues to be considered arise from attempts to improve schools".

The two issues which Mortimore then goes on to discuss are the impetus for change, and limits of change. Under the heading of the impetus for change he notes that simply knowing about the present situation cannot provide an adequate account of where change starts. Under the limits of change he notes that not all schools are equally well-endowed and, therefore, equally capable of improvement. However, this particular consideration is not one which arises from his earlier studies of school effectiveness.

Perhaps most remarkable is Mortimore's insistence that in spite of extensive studies of school effectivenesss, what is missing is a sound basis of well-developed theory. Mortimore (1998: 157) states that,

> "The third direction is whether researchers should now focus on the generation of theory rather than engaging in further, possibly repetitive, empirical work .... Nevertheless, it can be argued that it is

important that the findings of school effectiveness should now be incorporated into some kind of theoretical framework in order to gain the maximum value from all the empirical work, and to seek to identify underlying patterns. The problem is that the nature of the theoretical framework itself is the subject of a further set of options: whether to focus on individual learning and child development, or on institutional concerns, such as school management or change?"

Clearly Mortimore is not only pointing to the need for better theory, but is also pointing to that precise tension which lies at the heart of partial autonomy; whether the school should be studied as an institution or the learners should be studied as individuals, and how those two parts link together. While I do not suppose that Mortimore's answer to what more theory would look like would be exactly the same as mine, I find it very interesting that his critique of the methods, which he has done so much to develop, includes a number of elements which closely parallel the critique that I have offered of those same methods, and which I have offered of theory in research in Education Studies more generally.

Towards the end of his book Mortimore responds specifically to some criticisms which have been made of the work presented by him and colleagues over the decades. While he acknowledges the importance of critical discussion in developing academic studies, he is clearly bewildered, not to say hurt, by some of the criticisms which have been offered. For example, he notes (Mortimore, 1998: 322),

"Some critics accuse us of ignoring the observable processes of schooling. Elliot (1996), in particular, appears to believe that if the processes are 'good' then the outcomes will look after themselves (p.206). We dispute that on the grounds that educationalists still know very little about the relationship between teaching and learning for any individual student."

Mortimore goes on to argue that in his work on school effectiveness he and fellow researchers have spent a great deal of time looking at processes within schools.

However, the fact remains that in correlation studies there are only two kinds of variables; dependent variables, or that which is to be explained, and independent variables, or that which explanations are offered in terms of. It follows that even when Mortimore and his colleagues can include process variables, these must appear either as input variables, independent variables or output variables, dependent variables in the statistical methods that they use. Mortimore therefore rejects the notion that he has ignored process because he has examined process, and therefore fails to see the criticism that the theory which he has used does not allow for the inclusion of the study of process.

Similarly, he notes that a number of critics "accuse us of ignoring questions of equity." (Mortimore, 1998: 323). Again this clearly puzzles Mortimore who has spent a great deal of effort describing the distribution of opportunities within school with great accuracy. Equity in the sense of describing lack of equity or lack of equality has been the major focus of his work, but precisely because of the difficulty of getting from description to policy, his work does not come across as being motivated by a policy-orientated desire to remove inequality. Mortimore is caught on the horns of the dilemma that one cannot easily get from a detailed description of how things are to a rational prescription of what needs to be done.

Finally, Mortimore is perhaps most strongly stung by the accusation of ideological commitment (Mortimore, 1998: 324). Again Mortimore and his critics appear to be talking past each other; Mortimore regards himself as free of ideological commitment because he is determined to describe schools as they are, without fear or favour to any particular political grouping, whilst precisely that feature of his work and the difficulty of moving from description to prescription is what condemns him, in the eyes of his critics, to supporting the status quo, and therefore being essentially conservative. We are effectively being offered a choice by educational theorists between good descriptive work which does not have the points of purchase for developing policy, and policy orientated action which does not have the framework to accommodate good empirical and detailed work. The two sides in this methodological debate barely seem able to understand each other, as they each argue their own case.

I shall come back to those who advocate direct action and policy orientated solutions in the next chapter. For the time being this debate, as argued by Mortimore, points to very similar shortcomings in theory to those which I have set out towards the end of Chapter 1, and even indicates some of the solutions which I have entertained there. The difficulty of moving from good description to ethical and reasoned policy is of primary importance; in Mortimore's words it is "pivotal" how we get from school effectiveness to school improvement. It is also clear that single-centredness is an issue which comes up again and again in the context of Mortimore's debates. In one instance he expresses an opinion directly related to the issue of single-centredness (Mortimore, 1998: 327):

"Lauder *et al.* accuse school effectiveness research-ers of ignoring the argument made twenty years ago by Willis (1977) that 'working-class' students have often made a rational decision to reject 'compliance' for 'credentials'. This point is fair: most school effectiveness studies do start with the assumption that students want to succeed. If, for any reason, this is not the case, then many of the strategies of school improvement are likely to fail. The point is the one raised in the last chapter, by Geoff Whitty and

> myself, that the system needs to permit as many as possible to succeed – albeit at different speeds with different amounts of support and to different levels."

In effect this is a clear commitment to single-centredness that only success as defined by schools is going to be described as a success. And that only such success is going to be promoted by whatever means necessary.

We might compare this with an analogous situation from everyday life. Suppose that there are two routes to the city centre. One follows a main road, while the other involves cutting through back streets. In the rush hour, we would be surprised if all of the traffic was following one route. Nor would we be inclined to think that those following the 'wrong' route had been socialised into attitudes which predisposed them to follow the wrong route. On the contrary, we would expect both routes to carry traffic, and for the time taken to reach the centre along the two routes to be very similar. (If either route offered a major advantage, we would expect traffic to transfer to it until there was no further advantage).

In the same way, game theory (set out in detail in Chapter 6) offers the prospect of describing routes through the education system in a way which explains why people are following all possible routes, and explaining why certain proportions follow one route or another. It is important to the project of disconnecting the macro-level analysis from the individual-level that game theory does not make any prediction about the behaviour of individuals within the system.

Within a game theory approach, all possible routes are seen to make sense. One is seen as pathological or 'wrong'. This is in line with my own experience of talking to people making educational choices; they always appear to have good, which is to say, not pathological, reasons for following the path they do. Understanding why both outcomes to the choice make sense seems to me to come much closer to Weber's concept of *'verstehen'*, or 'understanding', than the traditional approach of

51

looking for explanations of why people take the 'wrong' route. Weber describes the method of 'understanding explanation' as:

> "on the one hand the conventional habits of the investigator and teacher in thinking in a particular way and, on the other, as the situation requires, his capacity to 'feel himself' empathetically into a mode of thought which deviates from his own and which is normatively 'false' according to his own habits of thought". (Eldridge, 1972: 28).

This ability to empathise with the value of a course of action which I would not follow myself is positively facilitated by the game theory model.

In conclusion we find that in spite of Mortimore's generally positive view of the approach to statistical survey methods which he has taken, we also find a surprising emphasis upon much the same shortcomings as I have pointed to in Chapter 1. There is at least the suggestion in Mortimore's work that the problems are a lack of well-developed theory, a difficulty of accommodating programmes of action or developing policy recommendations on the basis of descriptive models, and a hint that single-centredness is problematic. His work also focuses attention on a continual struggle with partial autonomy between levels of the education system, where he points out that we know something about the way in which organisation of schools is linked to effectiveness, but where we have rather more limited understanding of the way in which individuals learn. Although Mortimore's idea of what improved theory would be might not coincide exactly with mine there is a remarkable coincidence in our analysis of what is lacking in the present state of Education Studies.

CHAPTER FOUR: ACTION RESEARCH

Action Research is a broad church, which incorporates a number of approaches as well as internal debates. Its focus is generally the professional practice of the teacher, who reflects upon their own performance in order to clarify their concerns and improve their control.

> "Action research is inquiry or research in the context of focused efforts to improve the quality of an organization and its performance. It typically is designed and conducted by practitioners who analyse the data to improve their own practice." (NCREL, 2002)

This definition implies two quite different foci for what is called Action Research. The first is that it is focussed upon programmes of institutional change. The second is that it is focussed upon the critical reflections of a professional acting upon their own practice. There may be something like an assumption that these two processes are equivalent, but there is no consistent attempt to demonstrate the truth of such an assumption.

A Critique of Scientific Method

Notwithstanding such debates, Action Research is an important constellation of ideas, because it has been adopted by some UK government agencies, including the Department for Education and Skills (DES), Teacher Training Agency (TTA) and the General Teaching Council (GTC), as an appropriate vehicle for continuing professional development. In line with the general position adopted in this book, a critique of Action Research will be offered in this chapter, on the grounds that the focus on reflective professional practice is not necessarily conducive to the effective development and application of theory. In too many Action Research studies, research questions are addressed which cannot be adequately answered with the methods chosen.

However, Action Research does not exist in a vacuum. It is, to a great extent, a reaction to the current state of theoretical development in Education Studies. In particular, Action Research incorporates, or implies, a critique of large-scale survey methods, and statistical methods which aspire to being scientific. Using criteria such as reliability and validity to assess educational results, statistical methods have been employed which have emphasised the measurable, and have undervalued the individual and subjective experience of teaching professionals. In this chapter we shall see that the critique offered by Action Research of existing theoretical research is well-founded. But I shall go on to argue that, by giving no explicit place to the application of theory, Action Research encourages atheoretical studies, and consequently inhibits the development of theory.

Science itself has changed dramatically since the end of the nineteenth century. For the most part when people have tried to borrow from the physical sciences and develop the social sciences by that means, they have borrowed the notion of science as it was in the nineteenth century. I would argue that we can borrow much more fruitfully from the methods of the physical sciences if we incorporate many of the insights which have been developed through the twentieth century. But in particular I would argue that it is not sufficient simply to borrow willy nilly from the physical sciences. We must only borrow that which meets the criteria set out for good theory in Chapter 1.

Against this background of supposedly scientific studies in education, McNiff provides the following critique of what she describes as 'traditional research':

"Traditional research... is based on the principles of botany, that you successfully compare one plant with another. Scientists who believe in this sort of predicted knowledge apply the theory to people. People will behave, they say, in such and such a way if they are placed in controlled situations. So, depending on the stipulated conditions of learning, then a certain form of learned behaviour will be the product... Traditional research is all about scientific results which may be quantified, duplication of tests, replication of experiments, prediction of how the data will fall out. Action research is all about people explaining to themselves why they behave as they do, and enabling them to share this knowledge with others." (McNiff, 1992: 124)

McNiff sets out the clear opposition of Action Research to the framework derived from an objectifying and generalising scientific method which could be broadly described as positivism. She makes the case that individual observation of a single case can generate knowledge just as much as can experimental design or survey approaches to the study of education. In the light of what I have said earlier about scientific method in the role of theory in science, it is clear that this critique of supposedly objective methods in education is fully justified and absolutely necessary. The botanical model which McNiff criticises is, like Mill's description of it, drawn from a nineteenth century understanding of science. As has been noted in Chapter 2, it is an incomplete description of science in the twentieth century, and this may lead to some of the possible benefits of a scientific approach being overlooked. The root problem here is not that McNiff is wrong in criticising some rather arid, foolish and self-proclaimed scientific approaches to educational theory. The problem is that McNiff's answer, of using whatever methods are appropriate to a particular study, can lead to an undervaluing of theory as such.

The need to produce this polemic against, as I would see it, a misunderstood scientific method leads to an overstatement of the case that valuable knowledge can be generated from the study of the single instance. The fact of the matter is that we cannot even describe a single instance; as soon as we apply words to the situation, we are by implication generalising and drawing links and contrasts with other situations. If I start to describe my experiences in teaching a child a particular topic, I have already, by labelling the participants as myself and a child, made certain generalising assumptions about the relationship which holds. Also, in the verb 'to teach' I have implied certain relationships which are now to be found within that single situation but which draw upon experiences much more widely. The need to generalise is not an imperative which is unique to scientific method or to a positive scientific method. A need to generalise is a feature of the use of language itself.

What I am criticising in Action Research is not the emphasis upon generating knowledge through specific case studies or in the studies which a practitioner can conduct into their own practice. The critique which is offered of the supposed scientific method is perfectly legitimate and proper insofar as it goes.

McNiff adds:

> "Statistics-based tests will describe to me the situation as it is, without taking due account of the social and personal factors that make it so. They also stop at this point of description." (McNiff, 1992: 126)

She should perhaps say that they should stop at this point of description, since, as has been noted above, the real problems start when statistical methods are used to go beyond description and are used to identify causal models.

However, in trying to sort out a prognosis for future research, there is a difficulty in that, by using the term "social and personal factors", McNiff adopts the language of the statistical methods she rejects. We can imagine the statisticians coming back with the response, "It's all right now; we have included additional variables in our model to take into account the social and personal factors". (Indeed, we have seen Mortimore (pp.48-49) claiming to have included a study of process in very much these terms.) This would not satisfy me, and I am sure that it would not satisfy McNiff. However, the difficulty is that, in the absence of an explicit effort to reconceptualise educational theory, the assumptions of traditional research may be smuggled back in, either in the guise of familiar language or as 'common sense' assumptions.

The issue is not whether the critique offered by Action Research is correct but whether it places the balance in the correct position by undervaluing generalising theory, and focussing upon individuals researching and improving their own practice. There is a tendency, although not necessarily explicit in any theories of Action Research, to play down the value of the theory and, consequently, to leave theory unexamined. The result is that Action Research often, although by no means always, results in very detailed analysis of specific educational situations which are poorly theorised and in which theory is not examined particularly critically.

In the example I gave in Chapter 2 about the experience I had of working with twins, it might be argued that I was operating at that time in an Action Research mode. I was faced with particular aspects of practice which I then researched in theoretical terms and applied that theory in my own practice in order to develop a further understanding both of my own practice and of the theories involved. And in that sense I have absolutely no objection to Action Research where theory is introduced explicitly and critically. The difficulty arises when the study of practice is made an end in itself and leaves no room for the development of theory or for the study of theory. The consequence of any attempt at an atheoretical approach is that studies revolve around the application of received theory and poorly articulated theory. Since theory frames what we can describe in the first place, and, as I have argued elsewhere, removing theory from observations completely is impossible, the emphasis which is produced in much practitioner research leaves little room for the development of good theory.

A claim of Action Research, eloquently put by McNiff, is that individuals can examine, reflect upon and use as a source of evidence their own experience, normally professional experience, within educational settings. This experience is seen to be as valuable as that which is produced by external observers conducting educational surveys on a grand scale. In order to validate this kind of evidence McNiff needs to highlight the spurious nature of the claim to objectivity. She also needs to make plain that single case studies or individual experiences can be highly illuminating. It is not necessary, as Mill claimed, to look at various instances and to seek similarities and differences within those various different experiences. What every teacher knows, and what every learner knows, is that individual, one-off, unrepeatable events can be of critical importance to the educational process. McNiff's goal is to rehabilitate those individual experiences as the basis for the development of educational accounts and understanding. What I want to emphasise here is that McNiff's critique of the pseudo-scientific approach to the study of education is absolutely legitimate when directed against Mill's description of that scientific method. However, when taken more broadly, the Action Research agenda which is derived from that critique has some unfortunate consequences which hamper the development of theory in Education Studies. In particular, whether intentionally or by accident, the Action Research agenda undervalues the role of theory in developing our understanding of educational processes.

Although it is unfair to lay the worst excesses of such an approach at the door of any theorist of Action Research, the logical outcome of this approach finds its sharpest expression in the policy of the Department for Education and Skills (DES) and their grants for research conducted by teachers. In this programme the Department awards grants of £2,000 to individual teachers so that they can conduct research into their own practice. The aim of the Department is to achieve a collection of 500 word summaries of research by teachers in their own classrooms, which express the 'nuggets of wisdom' which can be applied by other teachers in their classrooms.

The political agenda which is being advanced here is that research into classroom practice is not an appropriate area for the application of theory and that those who favour theory – by implication academics in universities – have no place in the development of understanding professional practice in schools. Clearly in this case the agenda of the DES is coloured by a range of ambitions including the removal of the funding for educational research from other government agencies so that the DES becomes responsible for all aspects of education and can drive research in particular, policy-oriented directions. This is not a necessary consequence of the ideals of Action Research but is greatly assisted by the failure of Action Research to identify clearly a place for theory within Education Studies.

The Implications of the Critique

Such an approach is also assisted by the fact that Action Research highlights and privileges the role of the individual in understanding their own action. While that is a legitimate emphasis in itself, it has a tendency to de-legitimise the role of outsiders in understanding educational processes. The not necessarily logical but certainly corrosive corollary of this is that I am supposed to be unable to understand the practice of groups of which I am not a member. This will exclude me as a white middle-aged male from understanding the practices of youth cultures, of women, of minority ethnic groupings because I cannot enter into those practices as an active participant.

This has the unfortunate consequence that theory in Education Studies is in danger of becoming impossible, since no individual can have the range of experience which would allow them to generalise about the experiences of different groups. A moment's thought will show how damaging this must be. I do not need a theory to understand the activities of middle-class middle-aged white males because I have direct experience to fall back on and personal intuitions which I can use in developing that understanding. It is precisely where I do not have direct experience that I need theoretical constructs to help me to understand the experiences of others. I have a particular interest in theoretical approaches to political studies and to the management of policy because as an individual I lack those intuitive insights into how to behave politically to achieve results. Consequently, I need theory to compensate for intuitive understandings. In exactly the same way I need theoretical constructs of multiculturalism and affirmative action in order to enable me to understand and empathise with the activities and position of groups of which I am not a member.

The failure to give theory a pivotal position or even a clearly identified position within the research process leads to the development of particularly poor approaches to research. Practitioners within a practice-based tradition have difficulty in locating the work they are doing against a backdrop of other work which has been done before. The result is that the research questions are rarely clearly enough defined and the researchers may spend a great deal of time doing work which has been more carefully and adequately addressed by other researchers. At the same time those researchers are encouraged to adopt methods which are inadequate for the research questions which they claim they are trying to address.

It is one of the mysteries of life in education that quite large groups of individuals can show dramatic variation. For example, one would suppose that the young people coming into a school in any one year are, on average, very similar to the group who joined the school in the previous year. However, experience tells us that because of individual variation and because of differences in the way groups interact, one year's intake, even in quite large schools, can be very different from the year immediately before or immediately after. The educational experience of a professional practitioner will therefore vary considerably from year to year even though they are notionally doing exactly the same things with a similar group of pupils. However this fact makes it extremely difficult to separate the detail of the specific experiences from more generalisable statements about education.

On the other hand, a very great deal of work has been done on such aspects of education as differential performance of boys and girls in different subjects, the performance of twins or the performance of ethnic minorities within educational systems. Although these studies relate to relatively small differences between groups (and it is well to remember that intra-group differences nearly always exceed inter-group differences) the fact that very large numbers of people have been studied means that we do have some generalisable statements about the variation between these different groups. It would be unsound and almost certainly pointless for me to study the differences between boys and girls, or between different ethnic groupings, in a single class which I am teaching, in order to illuminate any question which has been studied at a more general level with more sophisticated tools. Although that background research may inform my professional practice and may help me sharpen what it is that I can study within my own classroom, merely ignoring the body of research which is available is not at all helpful. At the very least, this suggests that there is a need to engage with theory in practice-based study in order to identify an appropriate match between the questions being asked and the methods being used.

Novice researchers often find considerable difficulty with exactly this point. They conduct a literature survey but do

61

not know how that literature survey should inform a study of their own practice and therefore jump from a study of background theory to a detailed study of an individual case without any clear indication of how those two parts link together. We need to recognise that theory is not about establishing the truth but is about establishing a framework within which some questions can be answered, other questions can be ignored for the time being, and yet other questions are made unavailable for study. Then we can see that the literature survey should inform the way in which the study is developed in a creative and constructive way. My contention here is that the development of Action Research, which has criticised scientific approaches to Education Studies *'tout court'*, has managed to disconnect the relationship between theory and the study of practice, and is therefore damaging. And primarily it is damaging because it removes the role for theory in the studies which educational practitioners make of their own practice.

Once again, I want to stress here that the critique offered by Action Research of a Millsian approach to the science of Education Studies is entirely and totally correct and completely appropriate. I would wish to disavow as much as any action researcher an inductive approach to theory within Education Studies. The point that I have been making throughout this work is that science itself has moved on considerably since the end of the nineteenth century. Not least the physical sciences were overtaken by the revolution of relativity and more importantly from my own personal perspective from 1940s onwards operational research was developed within a scientific mathematical framework. What I am arguing here is that the critique which is offered of an objectifying, inductive and generalising science which is valid of 19th century social scientific views is not a valid critique of all possible insights that can be transferred from science to Education Studies. The very effectiveness and correctness of the critique offered by Action Research tends to make less likely a sensible rapprochement between theory and practice within Education Studies. The goal of this book is precisely to present a range of twentieth century scientific frameworks for consideration.

I have noted earlier that what needs explaining is itself subject to the theories that we adopt. What is important about theories is not so much whether they are true or false but what it is that they describe as in need of explanation. Thus, moving from an Aristotelian model of the world to a Newtonian model of the world, what needed explaining was the change in the speed of objects and not their motion itself.

We can see that deeply imbedded in statistical approaches and the apparently common sense notions which underpin them are a range of assumptions about what it is that needs explaining and how it should be explained. Game Theory models suggest that different things need explaining and the range of methods which are available for explaining them is also different. New models focus attention on different phenomena. I am suggesting that Game Theory models focus attention on elements which are of greater value to teachers and policy makers in practical circumstances than the models which have been adopted since the 1960s through to the present time.

What I have been arguing throughout is that a change in overall theoretical direction is needed, and that this must be based upon an understanding of the key ethical issues in developing theory. Educational theory must be recast in a re-imagination of the whole field, and of what it means to be an active agent in one's own education.

If this could be achieved by incremental steps, by the accretion of additional insights, then the programme of Action Research might be justified. But Kuhn has pointed to the dramatic difference between 'normal science' and 'scientific revolutions'. What is needed is a scientific revolution, while Action Research is, at best, an agenda for normal science.

There may be very little wrong with Action Research as such: its critique of the goals of an objective and objectifying science is accurate. However, the critique is beside the point as it is directed at an outdated model of the sciences. But it runs the risk of devaluing theory to the point where critical scrutiny of the prevailing paradigms becomes impossible, and where the task of re-imagining Education Studies cannot be achieved.

"You cannot step into the same river twice (or even once)." Action research, the study of individuals acting within this changing environment, addresses the question of what it means to learn.

Survey methods cannot tell us anything about that individual experience, because information about group behaviour cannot be tied precisely to individual incidents. As Mortimore finds out (1998: p 168) notes, some individuals may always "buck the trends". But by the same token, those individual experiences cannot add up to sound generalisations. This is why we need models which allow partial autonomy between levels.

Survey methods in Education Studies represent an attempt to produce a science of education which is measurable, repeatable, objective and secure. Based on the methods of the physical sciences, as understood at the end of the nineteenth century and expounded by Mill, statistical methods which stress validity and reliability are supposedly used to identify the specific causes of educational outcomes. The ultimate goal is a precise, descriptive account of education. Mortimore (1998) notes the limits of that achievement, and recognises that simply reproducing more of the same is unlikely to lead to the success of that project. McNiff offers a cogent critique of such supposedly scientific approaches.

Action Research addresses a different set of questions, aiming at a secure, prescriptive approach to what is to be done in an essentially ethical environment of education. The development of reflective professionals who apply moral judgement to the review of their own practice is seen as more important than developing a broader, descriptive understanding of how education operates in any larger sense.

Both approaches suffer from the weakness of not being able to accommodate the best of the alternative approach.

64

Survey methods cannot provide prescription, while the individual and ethical approach cannot accommodate adequate descriptive detail. What is lacking is a third approach, which might be described as 'technological'. There are negative overtones to the words 'technological' and 'engineering' as they imply a level of manipulation which is generally seen as reprehensible.

However, the technologist is interested in much more, and much less, than either the descriptive or the prescriptive approach. Description is necessary to shape the choice of means but cannot identify ends. Prescriptive methods can identify ends, but lack the framework for examining means which are likely to be effective in achieving those ends.

The technologist has to balance a range of extraneous elements, including cost, elegance, usefulness, which are not amenable to precise analysis of truth or ethics. In developing a technology of education, models are needed which allow for the incorporation of such a broad constellation of concepts into the analysis.

Looking to the physical sciences for precise models is not very helpful – a theory of technology has not been well developed, at least in part because scientists argue that they pursue the 'truth' and that it is for others to resolve the problems of application, and whether certain scientific solutions should be implemented. In education such a sharp division is impossible – witness Mortimore's argument that he has been concerned with equity and policy. A theory of the technology of Education Studies, or of how policy applications can be developed from research findings, will be more difficult than in the physical sciences. The importance of managing the transition from research to policy has been highlighted by criticisms offered of research in Education (NERF, 2000; Tooley, 1998). But without any clear models from the physical sciences, developing such a basis for policy will require considerable imagination.

CHAPTER FIVE: POSTMODERNISM

In this chapter I examine the influence of postmodernism and particularly the sense in which this acts as an obstacle to the development of theory ('grand theory' or 'grand narrative'). In general, postmodernism calls into question the usefulness, or even the validity, of the search for overarching theory. The absence of a central theoretical position makes it rather difficult to identify a collection of tenets which can possibly be described as 'postmodernism', but there are a number of influences and propositions which can be seen as making up the postmodern position.

For the purposes of this chapter, therefore, I will take as a starting point the work of Thomas (1997, 2002) as a statement of the postmodern position within education. Thomas puts forward a coherent argument against the use of theory in Education Studies and draws upon a range of authors including Althusser, Bourdieu, Feyerabend, Foucault and Kuhn who collectively make up something which approaches a canon in postmodernism.

Thomas (1997: 101) argues that,

"Theory in education is antagonistic to pluralism in ideas. With commitment to it, fertility is sacrificed to orderliness. What is needed is more 'ad hocery,' more thought experiments, more diversity."

His objection to theory is quite clear. It is perhaps important to note that there is quite a lot in Thomas' critique of theory with which I agree. What passes as theory in Education Studies at the moment is not something which we could hold up as an example. The principal difference that I have with Thomas is in terms of his conclusion. He concludes that we should avoid theory; I argue that what is needed is better and more explicit theory. For this reason it is worth examining his argument in detail to see why we should arrive at such different conclusions.

Thomas develops a three-pronged attack on theory. He argues that 'theory' is used to cover a wide range of activities not all of which should come under the general heading of theory. He argues that the pursuit of theory promotes the search for universal generalisations or regularities. And he argues, as in the quote above, that theory stands in opposition to creativity. I shall take each of these three strands of argument in turn.

'Theory' as a range of activities

Thomas (2002) describes the range of activities which come under the general heading of theory. These can be visualised as a spectrum ranging from, on the one hand, any kind of logical reasoning, through to explicit and abstract model building at the other end. He argues that simply thinking logically does not merit the word theory since labelling it in that way is no more than trying to ride on the coat tails of the prestige of scientific theory. His main focus for criticism is at the other end of the spectrum, those general and abstract theories which are used to describe practice and practical situations. Up to a point I have no quarrel with Thomas drawing attention to this distinction. He says (Thomas, 2002: 430): "Clearly in theory's form as thinking or reflection… there can be no charge against it." We are in agreement that thinking and critical reflection are of value under whatever banner they are conducted.

Thomas reserves his strongest criticism for the more abstract forms of theory building. That is where I do take issue with him and I will return to that point later. However, we need to note that a simple separation of theory and critical reasoning is not altogether possible.

When we build explicit models and develop well articulated theories we not only describe the situations which we find but we also build in a range of assumptions about what is to be explained and how events are to be explained. Theoretical models incorporate not only concepts which can be used in descriptions but pre-suppose certain articulations about how one theoretical entity can interact with others. One of the reasons why we have to be careful of sanctioning critical reflection in isolation is that there is a backwash from theory building into our use of every day language. Many of the inadequate models which are developed in the area of Education Studies are causal and are based upon a single centredness which I have criticised earlier. These particular pre-dispositions are not avoided simply by dismissing theory because many of those assumptions are also carried through in every day language. As soon as we start applying language to describe situations we import a whole range of theoretical assumptions. By describing a meeting as a lesson, or a person as a pupil, we build in a whole range of assumptions around the likely and possible interactions which take place within that setting. Those assumptions are more dangerous, not less, if they are smuggled in as common sense or are left unexamined. One of the reasons that I advocate an increased use of explicit theory in Education Studies is that framing propositions as theoretical models and constructs makes them more available for critical scrutiny. I do not believe that the problems of theory can be avoided entirely by putting theory on one side.

Theory as the search for abstract generalisations

Thomas (2002: 422) characterises the ends of the theoretical spectrum in terms of Althusser's *Generalities Two : General Thinking Tools* and *Generalities Three : Theory as Provisional Generalisations.* In a descriptive sense it is possible to talk in rather general terms of large populations. It is a fact in Western society that women tend to live longer than men and that middle-class children tend to receive more education than working-class children. That descriptive use of theory, however, is not the end of the story. Theoreticians often attempt to go beyond mere description and to develop models which will account for the mechanisms which are in operation. The least imaginative way of moving forward is to look for causal models which identify the factors which invariably lead to a specific outcome. The resulting understanding can well be described as 'generalities'.

Generalities of this sort are exactly what I have criticised in the current theory in Education Studies for being single centred, namely for presuming that there are general principles that if we find a group of people subject to the same causal factors they will inevitably respond in an identical way. But I have also tried to show that explicit model building could, and should, be able to address, or leave space for, human agency as is the case with models drawn from game theory, linear programming or chaos theory.

I conclude that when theorists move from descriptive models to look for those explanations of the mechanisms in operation theorists lack imagination and fail to apply some important precepts which derive from the fact that observed phenomena are human actions. Thomas concludes that it is the act of theorising itself which is at fault.

The most interesting human actions are those which do not rely on a chain of causal relationships. When I put a date in my diary to meet somebody on a day some months ahead, there is no traceable causal link between the conditions in which we make the appointment and the conditions in which it is later fulfilled. Honouring an engagement is an act of human will which cuts across any possible causal links which happen in between times. In moving from descriptive generalities to more effectively articulated theory, theory which is capable of accounting for human actions and theory which is capable of acting as the foundation for policy intervention, that I shall call manipulative theory (because it can form the foundation for manipulating future events), theorists in the social sciences and particularly in Education Studies have failed to make a break from the strait-jacket of the statistical methods they use for descriptive purposes. By describing the end of the spectrum of activities covered by the word 'theory', Thomas fails to see anything beyond Althusser's *Generalities Three*. I hope that the examples which I will provide from game theory and chaos theory give an indication of how abstract and explicit model making might operate to transcend that strait-jacket of generalising.

Theory as opposed to creativity

Thomas criticises theory as placing a steel band around those who embrace theory. It constrains their imagination and encourages them to force observations that they make in their practice into frameworks which they do not fit. One example that he draws upon is the work of Piaget (Thomas, 1997). He argues that Piaget's theory has encouraged researchers to ignore the evidence of their own working practice and to force it into patterns which are in accordance with the theory. That may, indeed, be true and it is one of the saddest commentaries on theory in the area of Education Studies that very many great educational innovators from Pestalozzi to Piaget, via Froebel and Montessori, have developed followings who have turned imaginative insights into educational experience into sterile formulae for classroom management. This misuse of theory is to be deplored, but it does not mean that the theory was wrong, much less that the original search for theory was misguided. But perhaps we should look in the case of those great innovators for the point at which their creativity is most obvious.

In Piaget's case the great imaginative leap which he performed was in looking at children's test performance in a completely novel way. Before Piaget's time, the vast majority of educationists had been interested only in the right answers produced by children on test papers. Piaget saw that by paying attention to the wrong answers he could gain critical insights into the thought processes of children. Specific wrong answers were an indication of specific lines of reasoning which the children were employing and that in turn led to the almost universally accepted insight that in order to teach anybody one needs to understand what they bring to the learning process. That critical and creative insight was not possible before Piaget and it was the impetus to develop theory which led Piaget to examine those questions in a structured and systematic way.

Perhaps, inevitably, there is a period which is less creative as researchers struggle to apply Piaget's theories to a range of complex phenomena, a period which Kuhn would describe as normal science. But creativity in the scientific process is most obvious in the period of a scientific revolution in which new theory is being forged and developed. If we discard not only theory but the aspiration to theory then we discard many of the stimuli towards more coherent and robust understandings of the practice in which we are engaged.

If the proposers of new theories are sometimes impassioned and have a tendency to exclaim, along with Newton, "I do not make hypotheses", they may perhaps be forgiven on the grounds that they have put a lot of effort into constructing what they now seek to make public. If their followers tend to believe them then they are clearly to blame for not recognising and keeping in mind that all theory is provisional and all theory must be subject to critical scrutiny at some point in the investigation. The correct defence against the rigidity of theory is not the rejection of theory as such, for as we have seen the rejection of explicit theory simply leads to the employment of implicit theory. The correct defence against the rigidity of theory is to keep in mind that all theories are wrong and that they are actually being used for a different purpose, namely to enable us to make and describe observations. I might go on to say that this excessive reverence for theory derives from failings in science education which give people the unrealistic view that science does indeed produce true theories and that the main value of theories is that they offer true descriptions. But in that connection Thomas again draws a rather different, and in my view, inexplicable conclusion. He criticises theory in the field of Education Studies for not being sufficiently like theory in the physical sciences:

> "Theory in properly conducted science, (that is properly conducted according to Popper) is open to attack, tenuous, and devised in such a way that it is falsifiable. By contrast, in education, theory is often taken as creed-like. There is the tendency not only not to treat theory as something to be refuted - or even as tenuous, as a loose statement of where we are now - but to treat it as a sacred text, something to be cherished and protected, as I have tried to show in the case studies of grand theory above." (Thomas 1997: 96).

It is true that Thomas then goes on to quote Feyerabend with approval: "There is not a single theory that is not in some sort of trouble or other". In general, however, Thomas appears to be saying that theory is acceptable in the physical sciences where it works, but unacceptable in Education Studies where it does not.

Thomas' proposal is a recipe for staying forever in the mess we are currently in. What would have happened if, in the seventeenth century, Thomas' counterpart had succeeded in persuading Hooke and Newton, Boyle and Descartes that the pursuit of theory was restricting imagination in the physical sciences? Without the impulse towards grand theory, research lacks the whetstone upon which to sharpen the reflection and critical evaluation which is necessary for improving how we understand educational practice.

Overall, then, I am in agreement with very much of what Thomas offers as diagnosis of the current state of educational research. Theory is not viewed as provisional or as appropriate for critical scrutiny and this was one of the criticisms which Tooley had raised in reviewing the research literature in education referred to in Chapter 1. Moreover, much of what passes as theory in the area of Education Studies is no more than some rather inadequate generalisations which are drawn together using descriptive statistics. As I have noted these tend to be rather implausible causal models which are single centred and which lack the ability to cope with human difference and human choice.

However, when it comes to prognosis Thomas and I part company. He suggests that the answer is to reject grand theory, or at least to leave it where it belongs in the physical sciences, and to embrace a diversity of inspirational and creative positions in relation to the study of Education Studies. I argue that what we should do is to borrow what we can from the physical sciences, not least the insight into the fallibility of theoretical frameworks and the need to examine them critically, and that what we need is more explicit and more imaginative theory building. The atheoretical framework presented by Thomas and the postmodern framework offered by him and others is a positive disincentive to the development of such theoretical frameworks. We see everywhere the encroachment of simplistic models from the medical field into the educational as 'common sense' theory fills the vacuum which is left by educational researchers. Thomas (2002) ends by laying at the door of theoretical concern a lack of commitment to political action and policy action:

> "As Richard Rorty (1998) notes, academics have since the mid-60s become so preoccupied with the weighty matters of theory and theorising – developing it and defending it, and doing what Anderson (1994) calls 'methodological policing' – that they no longer concern themselves with the mundane matter of reform and social justice....

Rorty contrasts many of today's academics with pre-60s reformers whose aim was principally to protect the weak from the strong." (Thomas 2002: 431 – 432)

The difficulty with this position is that if we embrace ad hocery and reject theory we are left with many incommensurate and pluralistic views on what should be done and no way of testing or choosing between them. In the absence of adequate theory there is no way to choose between policies other than violence, either symbolic or actual, and postmodernism has done much to produce the policy inactivity and the lack of coherent political will of which Thomas complains.

When Kuhn described the transition of the scientific community from normal science into the scientific revolution many elements had to be present, not least of which was a suitable candidate to replace the prevailing theory of the time. There has never been an occasion when a failing theory has simply been rejected and replaced by an absence of theory. A rejection of grand theory or grand narrative is essentially conservative because it must lead to the retention of the existing theories. And the existing theories in Education Studies are completely inadequate. That single centredness or what Thomas describes as a tendency towards generalities leads us to be concerned about how to deal with teaching mixed ability groups, for example. Nobody complains that they are watching a mixed ability football team or listening to a mixed ability orchestra even though it is patent that the collective performance is enriched by a diversity in the skills of individuals we are watching.

But single centredness and a tendency within education to seek uniformity and conformity will not simply wither on the vine unless those theories which underpin it are replaced by better and more humane theories. Postmodernism is as much an obstacle to effective reform as to the development of better theory.

CHAPTER SIX: GAME THEORY AND INDIVIDUAL CHOICE IN SCHOOLING

In this chapter I set out an alternative approach to the theory of educational choice which is based on models taken from game theory of two person games. This is radically different from the traditional approaches to theory of educational choice, in the sense that game theory provides a model of situations in which one would expect individuals to follow all of the routes through the education system which are available. Moreover, the game theory models suggest the proportions in which people will follow those routes.

This can be contrasted with other methods of approaching descriptions of social groups which start from the assumption that in order to describe the behaviour of a group, one has to understand what each individual is doing in it. In her book, *Realist Social Theory*, Margaret S. Archer (1995) suggests that there are two different ways in which social theorists fail to separate the two levels, the individual as agent and the broader social grouping. She suggests that social theorists tend either towards downward conflation in which they assume that everything is the responsibility of the individual agent, or upward conflation where they assume that the behaviour of the individual is completely explicable in terms of the social groups that they belong to.

Having identified this as the key problem of social theory, that theorists show a tendency towards either upward or downward conflation, Archer struggles to separate the two in what she calls a morphogenitic approach. In effect she introduces time as a variable which allows the separation through a sequence in which society in general shapes the behaviour of the individual, and cumulatively the later behaviour of individuals shapes the new society in which they operate. In the terms I have set out in Chapter 1, Archer has identified the need for partial autonomy between the different levels of analysis. Rather than find a mechanism which preserves this partial autonomy, she tries to circumvent the difficulty by introducing time delays. This does not, in fact, preserve partial autonomy, and produces an unconvincing solution to the problem which has been posed.

Game Theory and Policy

In this chapter I will try to present a model of educational choice based on game theory. In order to do that I am going to develop a particular model of game theory which is based upon the two-person zero-sum game, and specifically one variation of that which is known as a game against nature. This is going to be a difficult task because it is a model which is unfamiliar. Game theory was developed in the 1940s by von Neumann and Morgenstern, and has subsequently been used in engineering, micro-economics, management studies and a range of social settings. Along with linear programming and some other related topics it makes up the field of operational research (operations research in the USA) which are becoming widely used in economics. They remain relatively unknown in the field of Education Studies however. I am going to apply the game theory model to a particular educational choice - namely, the decision to stay on at school after the age of compulsory education - although by implication a similar model could be applied to various choices at different stages in the educational process.

The process of developing a model and applying it in a particular case is relatively lengthy and I will need to prevail upon the reader's patience to follow the argument right through.

In order to secure that patience it is perhaps sensible to start with an explanation of why this is a necessary process. Let me start with a clear statement of what it is that needs to be explained. In the United Kingdom at the age of 16 pupils make a decision whether they will leave school or stay on to upper secondary education. A very large number of studies exist which demonstrate quite conclusively that on average staying on to upper secondary education is beneficial in terms of expected lifetime earnings. On average those who stay on at school earn more over their lifetimes than those who chose to leave school. Traditional economic theory would therefore lead us to expect that every child should choose stay on at school post 16.

However, in practice, we know this is not what we see in the educational system. Some children choose to stay on at school, while others choose to leave. Faced with the phenomenon that some children choose one route while others choose another, a traditional approach would be to look for those predisposing factors or elements in the child's background which lead them into staying on or leaving. The traditional assumption is that an identical group of people will all make the same decisions. The researcher's task is therefore to identify two groups on some criterion or some factor which can be separated to enable comparisons between those who stay on at school and those who leave school.

The argument developed here follows two broad lines. The first is that a satisfactory model of choice has to explain why an otherwise identical group of people should follow two different routes through the educational system. As has been explained earlier, this is an important feature of the model because it is that feature which allows one to retain a sense that the choices really are meaningful and that the human beings involved are exercising their own judgement and free will.

The second line of argument is that the model developed actually has some features which conform to the observed results in a way which the traditional models do not. The game theory model thus offers two attractive features which commend themselves for our consideration. In the first place, it permits the re-entry of free will and human agency into the description of educational behaviour, and in the second it explains some features of the way people behave which are not readily explained using other models.

I am not the first or only researcher to have looked at game theory models in describing educational behaviour. Raymond Boudon (1986) has also used game theory models and has explained why those models are attractive to him. His key point is that such models allow one to take into account the intentions and purposes of individuals and therefore permit us to examine forward or future-oriented behaviour. By implication this allows us to look at the moral and ethical actions which are being taken by those we observe. He notes that attempts to describe choices only and entirely in terms of pre-existing conditions are generally sterile and do not allow us normal understanding of why people behave in the way that they do. Boudon (1986: 43) argues that,

> "If motivation is infathomable and behaviour varies in a simple way according to the social characteristics of agents, does this not mean that the former should be ignored and the latter restricted to the study of co-variations between social characteristics and behaviour? A conclusion of this kind is clearly incompatible with the Weberian model, which presupposes that the subjectivity of the actors will be reconstructed".

If a behaviour, however bizarre it appears on the surface, does not serve some present purpose it is unlikely, in Boudon's view, to persist. It will never be satisfactory to say that a person behaves in a particular way because they have been infused with some dysfunctional beliefs or attitudes. If their current behaviour does not serve a useful function it will very soon die away. In Boudon's (1986: 31) words:

"In (Weber's) view, observers _understood_ the action of an observed subject as they can conclude that in the same situation it is quite probable that they would act in the same way".

In that sense introducing the game theory model raises a different set of questions. Instead of asking why people persist in doing something which is clearly dysfunctional, we are prompted instead to ask what purpose this apparently dysfunctional behaviour actually performs for those who are doing it. Even posing the question in this way offers some clear advantages in the sense that it shows the limitations of the models which are usually employed. However, to see more fully the implications of turning the question of choice in education around I will need to develop the game theory model more fully.

Bacharach (1976: 34-37) sets out what he understands by a game. The word 'game' should not be understood to mean that the decisions being made are something frivolous. What is required to be a game in the sense of game theory is that there should be one or more players who are assumed to make particular plays. At the end of each play the outcomes are well defined in terms of the combination of plays which are made. All of this should be known to the players, and the players should exercise logic in their decision-making processes.

This restricted meaning of the word 'game' in terms of game theory means that many of the things which we consider games, such as football or rugby, are not games in the sense of game theory, because the result is not certain once the strategies of the players are known. Games such as chess or draughts are games in the sense of game theory, because the outcomes depend only upon the combination of strategies chosen by the players. Game theory has also been applied to other real life situations of extreme seriousness, such as decisions of strategy in war, in labour negotiations and in micro-economics. The word 'game', then, is not intended to imply something frivolous.

Baseball is not in the game theoretical sense a game, although game theory has been applied to various aspects of it, as when the managers of both sides have to decide whether to choose a left-handed or a right-handed pitcher and left-handed or a right-handed batter. This is an important distinction because it means that what is being sought in the analysis of baseball is not that game theory is true, nor that it accurately describes some aspect of the game of baseball, but that game theory can be used to make sense out of the options which face a manager in making particular choices.

Two Person Zero Sum Games

The archetypical game in game theory can be relatively easily understood by considering a game known as 'Mora'. 'Mora' involves two players, each of whom has to make a decision in ignorance of the decision of the other. Each of them holds out either one or two fingers under the table, so that the other player cannot see.

The two players then simultaneously reveal their fingers to show how many they have extended. If the total number of fingers extended is odd, player A wins; and if the total number of fingers is even, player B wins. Supposing that they play for a simple stake, where whoever loses pays the other a penny, then we can describe the outcomes in a simple pay off matrix as shown below.

Figure 6.1: Simple pay-off matrix for a zero–sum game.

		Player A	
		One Finger	Two Fingers
Player B	One Finger	- 1	+ 1
	Two Fingers	+ 1	- 1

The pay off matrix shows the gain for player A; a gain for A is a loss for B

The point about the game theory is that there is not one right way of playing 'Mora'; there is not, in game theoretical terms, a pure strategy which is the best way of playing. If a player decides always to hold out one finger then his or her opponent can always win by choosing the number of fingers to hold out appropriately. In order to play 'Mora' effectively one has to play a mixed strategy of sometimes holding out one finger and sometimes holding out two. Because the winnings of one player are exactly equivalent to the losses of the other player, this kind of game is called a zero-sum game, or non-co-operative game.

Game theory suggests that there is a 'solution' to a game such as 'Mora'. In this example the solution is fairly simple; that each player should play one finger exactly half of the time, and that they should randomise their choices so that their opponent cannot guess what their next choice will be. However, if we alter the figures that appear in the pay off matrix, the solution changes in ways which may not be intuitively obvious.

Suppose that we change the pay off matrix so that the benefits in each case are as shown in the modified table shown below.

Figure 6.2: Pay off matrix for modified game of Mora

		Player A	
		One Finger	Two Fingers
Player B	One Finger	-1	+1
	Two Fingers	+5	-1

Here the reasoning is rather different because player A has one outcome which is very much preferable to the others. That is to say, a win where he holds out one finger and his opponent holds out two fingers is much better for him than the alternative win. Similarly, that same combination of fingers represents a major loss for player B. We would therefore expect player B to play that option with less frequency and it also follows that player A will move away from that option in order to capitalise upon the fact that player B has changed his strategy. Standard texts on game theory give solutions to the pay off matrix as follows.

Figure 6.3: A linear programming interpretation of the modified game of Mora

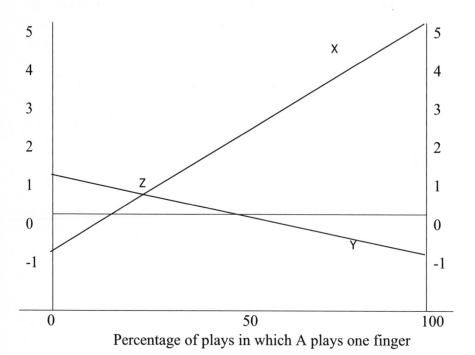

Percentage of plays in which A plays one finger

Line X represents the gains for A if B always plays two fingers. Line Y represents the gains for A if B always plays one finger. It follows that point Z represents the best that A can secure without the co-operation of B; B cannot force A's gains down if A can get to point Z. A can get to point Z by playing one finger 16 per cent of the time.

There is a paradoxical result here, which is that players will tend to move away from those options where the spread of the difference between their winnings and their losses is larger.

They will move towards the option where the spread between their winnings is smaller.

There is an interesting corollary to the solution of the game, which is that if a player is playing the optimum mixed strategy, then it actually does not matter what their opponent does. The optimum strategy represents a kind of insurance policy, or a basic minimum, which can be secured without the co-operation or any understanding of what the opponent is doing. This is described in the literature as the 'minimax' solution.

Games Against Nature

Version of zero-sum games is called 'Games Against Nature'. This model of zero-sum games was extended in classical studies by Davenport (1960) to describe the behaviour of people in uncertain situations. In Davenport's study, he examined the behaviour of a fisherman in the West Indies. The particular fishermen in question had to decide on any particular day whether they were going to put their lobster pots inside the reef or outside the reef. The other player, who Davenport described as Nature, for obvious reasons, had to decide whether to make a strong tidal current run or not to make a strong current run. The consequence of a strong tidal current was that all those fishermen who had put their lobster pots outside the reef lost their lobster pots and did not catch any fish. On the other hand, if a strong current did not run those who put their lobster pots inside the reef caught small and inferior fish and were unable to compete in the market place with those who had put their lobster pots outside the reef.

In analysing the behaviour of the fisherman, Davenport imposed a condition in his model analogous to that in the game of 'Mora', that the fisherman had no way of knowing whether a current would or would not run on a particular day. Using arbitrary figures for the economic losses, if lobster pots are washed away, and for the profit in the market place for bringing in the best quality catch on a particular day, one can arrive at a pay off matrix, something like the one illustrated below:

Figure 6.4: Fisherman's game against Nature

		Nature	
		Tidal Stream	No Tidal Stream
Fishermen	Inside Reef	3	1
	Outside Reef	-2	5

The pay off matrix above is sufficient to model the appropriate actions of the fishermen. This is that the fishermen would put some of the lobster puts inside the reef and some of their pots outside the reef and that the proportion of pots that they put inside or outside could be relatively easily estimated from the pay off matrix according to a solution of the type just calculated. That was indeed the behaviour of the fishermen that Davenport observed.

It follows from the concept of the 'minimax' solution that fishermen who have found the ideal mixed strategy will get exactly the same benefits whatever the current does and as a result of that they can insulate themselves from the vagaries of nature. Again, it is important to note what the model does not do. It does not say whether an individual fisherman would be well advised to split their lobster pots in accordance with the set proportion, or whether they would be better advised to put all their lobster pots outside the reef one day and inside the next and allocate days according to the solution. The actual behaviour is still left poorly described, or rather, is not determined by the solution of the game. What is described by the solution of the game pay off matrix is a long-term strategy which the fisherman can employ in order to secure a minimum level of returns over the long run.

Now I want to examine a case where such a model has been applied in an educational context. In 1971, I published a paper which analysed young people's choices on leaving school or staying on at school as a game against nature. The argument is that the young person makes a decision to stay on at school or to leave, but that certain other events, which are beyond the control of the young person, take place in order to effect their eventual success in their career, whether that is in school or out of school. In effect, I conceptualise the decision to leave school or to stay on at school at 16 as a game against nature in which the young person could be successful, or unsuccessful, through either of the two routes which are available to them. A game pay off matrix can be seen below where A is bigger than B and D is bigger than C.

Figure 6.5: General Matrix for Game against Nature

		Nature	
		I	II
Young Person	Stay at School	A	B
	Leave School	C	D

In order to put some figures into this pay off matrix, I took original data from the National Child Development Survey (NCDS). This related to their choices at 16 and their eventual income at the age of 23. I also restricted the study to those who had three or four passes at O level (GCSE) or equivalent - i.e. I excluded those who were so well or so poorly qualified that their decision may have seemed obvious. To get some approximation of the range between their winnings and their losses by following each path, I took the top five per cent and the mean of the income distribution. This gave the pay-off matrix shown below for one group (middle-class boys):

Figure 6.6: Pay off matrix for middle-class boys

| | | Nature | |
		I	II
Young Person	Stay at School	£100.53	£74.44
	Leave School	£84.58	£190.88

There are some obvious shortcomings with the approach that had been adopted in developing this game theoretical model of student choices at 16 plus. In the first case, because the NCDS is a longitudinal study, the figures that are used in the pay-off matrix are figures which related to seven years after the decision has been made, and it is therefore not necessarily representative of the actual choice that the young people faced. Moreover, it is not absolutely clear that one should be using actual figures, as opposed to the pay-off matrix as imagined by the participants or agents making the choice in the first place. An alternative way of dealing with this would be to ask young people aged 16 their perceived expectations from each course of action, supposing that they were successful or unsuccessful. I have tried this second method also, but it proves to be rather difficult to get reliable figures, given that the question which one is asking is a hypothetical one; if you take this course of action and if circumstances behave in a particular way, what do you expect your pay-off to be? It is not easy to see how such results can be compared.

However, what this case clearly illustrates is that data as currently collected in a large-scale survey, such as the NCDS, is not collected with a view to examining the range of risk which people face, and therefore is not easily adapted to a model which is unconventional such as the game theory model. This may seem surprising but the standard models which are used in social scientific analysis are shaping the way in which data is routinely collected. The type of analysis which the NCDS has been used for, and for which it is ideally suited, is a correlation analysis, in which one tries to identify which features of childhood background, for example, predispose children to leave school at 16 plus.

These correlational models offer an alternative way of interpreting the data to the one which has been offered here. And on the basis of empirical results, it is difficult to say which is the more accurate description of the phenomena.

However, what I am claiming here, is that the game theory model offers some interesting insights into aspects of the patterns of staying on and leaving school at age 16 plus which are not directly addressed by correlational models. More importantly, the game theory models provide a way of understanding why both leaving and staying on are sensible strategies in terms of developing a future career. In many years as a teacher, I have never felt that a person aged 16 took the decision to leave school or to stay on at school at 16 plus lightly. Nor did I think that I was seeing a large number of people who were making the wrong choice. What the game theory model provides is a framework within which one can see those who leave and those who stay on as making a strategically sensible choice. The important question - and it remains an important question for society and governments at large - is the extent to which circumstances produce a larger or smaller proportion of young people following one route or another. At this point it is appropriate to reflect upon the standard, 'scientific' approach to analysing this data, which is to look for correlations. For example, one might analyse the data to suggest that some variable, such as class background or education of parents, pre-disposes young people to leave school at 16 rather than to stay on. Such a result is bound to be approximate and this leads to a step-wise regression analysis in which one variable after another is taken as pre-disposing young people to leave school at 16 plus. However, the results are always provisional in the sense that no step-wise regression analysis has ever produced a precisely accurate description of what it is that might pre-dispose a person to leave school at 16 plus.

In theoretical terms, this is taken into account by suggesting that there is 'an error' which is not accounted for in the statistical method. We can perhaps see that this is an example of an approach which has been most accurately described by Bassey (2001) as a fuzzy generalisation, in which the hope is that one can, by increasing accuracy in the variables which one includes, eventually approach an answer.

We are saved from the problem of worrying about what would happen if we ever had a perfect regression and a perfect explanation of why young people leave school at 16 plus because it has never happened. If we envisage the theoretical possibility that we could identify all of those factors which predispose people to leave school at 16 plus, then we would be left with a rather grey theoretical problem. This is that we would have a perfect and deterministic model of why people behave in a particular way and this would be in contradiction with the ethical principles which are set out in Kant's *Critique of Practical Reason*, and which I have set out in Chapter 1.

At the heart of such approaches and the heart of Bassey's fuzzy generalisation is the notion that there is in the end one best way of answering the question, "Should I stay on at school?". I would describe the key feature of such regressions and of Bassey's description of fuzzy generalisations as a 'single centredness' - a tendency towards an ultimate truth which we are unable to achieve at the moment.

In contrast, what the game theory model offers is a 'multi-centredness'. It explains the decision which is being made but makes explicable and reasonable both possible outcomes. We cannot say that those who have chosen to leave school at 16 plus have been socialised, have been disadvantaged, have been misled, or in some other way have an aberrant behaviour. Instead, what we focus on is the fact that a group of people appear to be employing a mixed strategy and the game theory model directs us to certain features, in particular what the mix in the mixed strategy is. This is more productive in policy terms. This seems to me to be crucial; the model incorporates an explicit recognition of the agency of the individuals who are involved.

What is understood by a single play in a game is an area which is not addressed by game theory, and there is at the heart of the game theory model a failure or a lack, or a proscription which in effect leaves a place for an ethical or moral understanding of human behaviour. Again, I cannot answer for everybody, but in my own case. I would say I have made certain choices in moving through the educational system and that I would find it perfectly reasonable to understand those choices in terms of a game theory model. I happened to make particular choices but those choices were not determined by the circumstances in which I faced that choice, although they were clearly shaped by those circumstances.

Mixed Strategies

The key to understanding the possibilities which are offered by game theory lies in the notion of mixed strategy. In a game pay off matrix where no one strategy dominates, there is a theorem which states that a mixed strategy will dominate. A mixed strategy involves playing more than one of the pure strategies with a particular probability.

Perhaps an agricultural example can illustrate the features of the model further. In a study of the growing of maize in Tanzania, agricultural engineers and community educators observed the way in which peasant farmers planted maize. They first spread the maize onto the surface of the ground and then ploughed the ground. The result was that the maize seeds would be distributed at different depths in the soil.

The agriculturists decided that it would be better if all seeds were planted at the 'optimum' depth so that a maximum harvest and profits could be achieved. As a result, they instructed the peasant farmers to plough the ground first and then plant the seeds at a particular depth of, say, 5cm. When the plants had started to grow, and when they had reached a height of 10 or 15cm above the ground, the weather changed and there was a short period of drought. The outcome was that all the plants, which were at the same stage of development, were killed off by the drought.

If we look at what the peasant farmers were doing originally, we find that their strategy was to plant maize seeds at different depths. The outcome of such planting is that some of the plants germinate earlier, some later. Caught by a sudden drought, some of the plants are killed off, but those at a greater depth which have not yet fully developed are left in the ground to develop at a later stage when weather conditions are suitable. In effect, the peasant farmers were adopting a mixed strategy of positioning their various seeds at different levels in the ground so that they would grow under different conditions.

The agriculturists were right in asserting that, given optimum conditions, a maximum yield could be achieved by making sure that all the seeds were at the 'correct' depth. What they had not taken into account was the fact that the environmental conditions were uncertain. By playing a mixed strategy rather than a pure strategy the peasant farmers were ensuring a return against any behaviour which the weather conditions might impose upon them.

A further theorem in game theory says that the return from the optimum mixed strategy will be the same whatever the other player chooses to do. One can therefore see the behaviour of the peasant farmers as perfectly rational in providing a security level, or insurance level, of return on their planting whatever the weather did. This may not have been as high as the return which the agricultural engineers could achieve in optimum conditions, but it was a safeguard against the capriciousness of nature and weather conditions.

One of the consequences of looking at mixed strategies is that it moves one away from (I would say moves one on from) the view that there is one best strategy or one best way of dealing with a particular situation. The mixed strategy explains why and how dividing one's effort between two different strategies can be advantageous. Looked at from a game theory perspective, the behaviour of the peasant farmers served a particular function, namely, securing a certain level of crop whatever the conditions. This was important to them in terms of subsistence farming in providing a living for them rather than being focussed upon the production of a profit in the market by selling surplus grain. The perspective of the external advisors was that the primary purpose was to produce the maximum profit by sale of surplus product, and therefore they saw the behaviour of the peasant farmers as aberrant or in some way deviant from appropriate behaviour.

In education we are only too liable to describe the behaviour which does not conform to our expectations as in some way counter-productive or aberrant. When young people leave school at 16, when girls give up the study of science or when other educational choices are made, we tend to label those behaviours as problematic rather than trying to understand exactly what purpose those behaviours serve in terms of the conditions in which the young people find themselves.

I would argue that the game theory model gives us an opportunity to develop two dimensions which are not available if we insist upon the notion that there is only one best way of responding to every situation. The first dimension is that the model provides us with a tool which enables us to have an understanding of what the participants might be trying to achieve or what they might be seeing as their own best interests in a particular circumstance. I would argue that this takes us much closer to what Weber has taken as a major premise in advancing social sciences, that we should develop an understanding *("verstehen")* of the people who are being studied. The second dimension which the game theory model permits us to develop is precisely an ethical one of a non-judgemental description of what people are doing in particular situations. I think that this goes some way toward legitimising the notion that an external observer can impose the framework of analysis upon those people whose behaviour is being studied.

In both of these respects the game theory model comes closer to what I believe to be in my own direct experience of people making choices in educational contexts. I have seen young people and adults deciding to join programmes, to work hard on programmes, to leave programmes or to get by on programmes with minimal effort, and in all cases they appear to be able to provide an explanation which makes perfectly good sense in terms of what it is they hope to achieve. I think back, for example, to a very early experience with a 15 year old who was not interested in studying physics. When I asked him why he was not interested in studying a subject which would be of great vocational value to him, he simply answered that his intention was to leave school at 16 to become a taxi driver eventually, and that by the time he was my age he would own a fleet of taxis and be much better off than I was. I have to say that explanation and aspiration made perfectly good sense in the terms in which he set it, even though he was choosing to do something which I regarded as unwise, namely to drop out of education at the age of 16.

What the game theory model does is to focus our attention on the fact that there is more than one way in which to develop a future, an identity and an occupation and that all of them appear to make perfectly good sense to the participants in a subjective sense. All of our theories in education have been simplistic in the sense that they have focused upon an explanation of the one correct way of doing things. It may be argued that that in itself is a simplification of conventional analyses in education. But I would suggest that what we are normally doing in traditional analyses, when we confront the situation where a certain group of young people are leaving school against our own judgement, is trying to find explanatory factors, such as class or gender, which can account for that 'aberrant' behaviour. The game theory model allows us in a more sophisticated way to address the question that multiple approaches are not only possible but make perfectly good sense.

Again it is worth stressing that the notion of a mixed strategy does not say anything about individual cases. Indeed the interpretation of single plays within a game theory framework is highly problematic, and is addressed in the game theory literature. What one can see in a general sense is that a mixed strategy does not dictate that this particular maize seed should be planted 3cm below the ground and that particular seed should be planted 10cm below the ground. Rather, the game theory model addresses a whole distribution. Within that distribution there is scope for individual choice or individual selection. Again, in the case of educational choices, the game theory model will describe and perhaps elucidate why 70 per cent of an age cohort leave school or attend a particular kind of educational institution and 30 per cent take some other course, but it does not say anything about which individuals will be likely to follow which course.

Overall then, the concept of a mixed strategy permits us to provide a description of the behaviour of aggregates of individuals while saying nothing about the behaviour of specific individuals. It is that feature of this model which means that it can be applied to groups without contradicting the requirement that we respect the free will and individuality of people being studied. In this curious way, even though this model is derived from the physical sciences, it does not carry the same overtones, as the simple reductionist approach, for example, of explaining educational choice in terms of genetic disposition towards particular areas of study.

The other important feature of game theory models, as set out previously, is that they permit partial autonomy between the various different levels of understanding. They say something about the group but they do not determine what individuals are doing. This is an important feature of desirable theoretical frameworks which will recur throughout this book.

However, even using the rather limited data which we have available from the NCDS, some interesting issues emerge. If we look at the position of boys from working-class backgrounds and contrast it with those from middle-class backgrounds, the issues are raised in particularly stark format. The highest mean earnings and the highest earnings for the top five per cent of working-class boys all result from staying on at school. It must be remembered that this is the exact opposite of results from middle-class boys, and that one expects the reward for staying on at school to be better for the middle-class. But again, staying on at school is riskier for working-class boys and when the figures are put into a game matrix the model suggests that we would expect only 50 per cent to stay on at school. At one level, this does not need explaining in terms of games against nature. The riskier option is less attractive and that means that, for working-class boys, leaving school is more attractive as a risk avoidance strategy, while for middle-class boys, staying on at school is more attractive as a risk avoidance strategy.

In terms of classic theories of economic return and our expectations that people will choose the most lucrative option on average, these results certainly do need explaining. The use of the game theory model highlights things which are paradoxical in the current imagination of educational theory and which need further investigation.

This account of a game theory model of student choice ought to be enough to give an indication of how adopting new models can address some of the moral features of describing individual behaviour and also indicates some other areas where further work would be desirable. The nature of theories which we hold shapes the kind of data which we collect. The current models which are used in educational theory make it extremely unlikely that the data necessary to test games theory models will become available in the near future, unless deliberate steps are taken.

As developed here, the game theory model shows how the circumstances of a group of people (working-class or middle-class boys in this example) can shape and frame the decision of the individual without determining it. The game theory model, and particularly the notion of a mixed strategy, allows us to move away from single-centredness and towards a relative autonomy between the behaviour of the individual and the behaviour of the group.

CHAPTER SEVEN: LINEAR PROGRAMMING AND SOCIOLOGICAL LAWS

In Chapter 8 I will set out an example of how linear programming could be used to analyse a policy situation. In this chapter I will look at the theoretical foundations of linear programming and explore the relationship of this approach to other pragmatic frameworks for understanding educational studies. In particular I want to look at the notion of sociological laws which Holmes (1981) took from his reading of Popper as a basis for structuring an understanding of comparative education studies.

In this chapter linear programming is used as a way of understanding institutional policy within a policy framework set by government. Again, the emphasis is upon using theory as a framework for the description and analysis of non-deterministic relationships in education. And again, the technique develops the idea of partial autonomy by focussing attention upon the ways in which individuals (or individual institutions) are constrained, but not determined by, the environment within which they operate.

Linear programming involves drawing lines around the areas where workable solutions can be found. Each line represents a constraint upon solutions; on one side of the line a policy will work, and on the other side of the line it will not. In Chapter 6, linear programming techniques were used to find a solution of the game 'Mora' (Figure 3.3) The mathematical basis of linear programming is therefore closely related to that of games. However, in this section I move on to look at the use of linear programming in its own right as a tool for analysing policy issues in education.

I first came across linear programming as a technique when I was a young engineering student analysing electrical circuits. The archetypical use of linear programming is in defining the working conditions for a transistor in an amplifier stage. In this case, fairly well-defined variables are available in the voltage and current which are applied to the transistor in that situation. These can be shown in a graph of voltage against current as shown below. The circumstances in which such a transistor will fail can be fairly clearly defined. For example, manufacturers typically specify voltage and current which must not be exceeded. These are shown on the Figure 7.1 respectively as the lines AB and CD. However, a third condition also normally applies. This is that there is a limit to the power which can be dissipated within the transistor. The power, the product of the voltage multiplied by the current, must not exceed a fixed value. This results in a third boundary to the working conditions of the transistor, represented by the curved line EF on the Figure. We can therefore be relatively sure, as a designer of electrical circuits, that the transistor will function adequately provided that we do not exceed the three boundaries that the manufacturer of the transistor has specified.

One further lesson should be taken from the engineering applications of linear programming before we move on to look at it as a technique that is applicable to educational policy. This is that if the transistor is taken beyond the boundaries of its appropriate working conditions it will fail, but the way in which it will fail will depend upon which boundary it is taken across. Taking the transistor across line AB will have very different results from taking the transistor across line EF. (Taking the transistor across line EF produces excessive heat in the transistor, and we would expect a transistor which had crossed this constraint to show considerable heat damage. Such overheating would probably not be evident for a transistor which crossed constraint AB.)

Figure 7.1: The operating conditions of a transistor

Voltage (V)

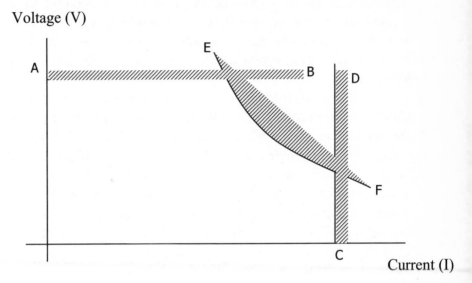

Sociological Laws

Holmes (1981) argued that studies of educational systems should be based on sociological laws in the form, "If we do this, then that will follow". Of course, from what I have said before, the reader will understand that I do not intend the term 'sociological law' to be imbued with that kind of certainty which once might have been attached to laws of physics. 'Sociological law' is no more than a hypothesis which enables a study to be conducted.

However, sociological laws are important because they provide the social policy maker with a framework for linking means with ends. They provide a hypothesis that the mechanisms of educational institutions function in particular ways. They specify the kinds of actions which will produce the results which the policy makers desire.

In this sense, sociological laws provide the link between the descriptive statistics of the large-scale survey methods and the innovation-driven methods of Action Research. They make possible a technology of educational policy as opposed to a science or art of education. Indeed, it would be reasonable to argue that it is an absence of sociological laws which accounts for the lack of interest which policy makers have for Education Research.

The difficulty which arises in connection with both Holmes' work and the work of Popper on which he draws is that the sociological laws proposed are actually extremely facile. There are no sociological laws which would merit a great deal of study. At one level, that is exactly the problem which I am trying to address in this book, namely, the lack of progress in discovering anything which could be regarded as a basis for technology of policy in Education Studies in spite of centuries of study. There is no basis or agreed framework which can be used for analysis, and upon which subsequent studies can be based.

At a personal level this is also a problem which I have come across having been challenged by a friend at a conference when presenting a paper on sociological laws to indicate any such laws that I had in mind. The answer is that there are relatively few which could be regarded as in any way sophisticated. There are, however, a number of assumed sociological laws, the most obvious of which is, "If we provide more resources for activity X, the likelihood of activity X happening will increase". In Chapter 8 I will be developing an example that suggests that even the operation of this sociological law may not be as straightforward as it appears. What I am going to do in this chapter is to look at how models developed from linear programming can be extended to create such sociological laws.

The other theme which I am developing through the use of models from game theory and linear programming is that of relative autonomy. That is to say, relative autonomy permits one to speak of either group activity or individual activity without assuming that the one is determined by the other. In game theory it was possible to talk of individual choices making up patterns of group behaviour without any assumption that the choices of individuals were determined. Similarly with linear programming it is possible to look at general guidelines of policy which set constraints on individuals and individual institutions while leaving considerable latitude in the individual actions, as those agents respond to the circumstances in which they find themselves. Determinism is not generally a feature of the systems that are described using game theory and linear programming. In this way it is possible to use these models to avoid what Archer (1995) describes as upward or downward conflation.

In chapter 8 I will set out a linear programme model of the funding system of institutions of higher education in the UK from the earlier 1990s. Elsewhere I have shown that this simple model could be formalised into the normal mathematical notation of linear programming (Turner and Pratt 1995). The mathematical formalism is not important for this explanation apart from noting that, because it is possible to express policies in mathematical notation, a number of theoretical consequences are available in a linear programming analysis. I want to note two particular consequences one of which I will use and the other of which I will deliberately avoid using. The first, which I shall be avoiding, is the 'objective function'; the second, which I shall be using, is the concept of a shadow price.

Let me take an example to illustrate the use of linear programming. A common problem which is analysed using these techniques in an engineering environment is the use of two different production processes to produce machined products. In an educational context this might be similar to making a decision to use staff to teach classes, or to use educational software as an alternative to the use of contact time for staff. By appropriately using a mix of inputs the desired level of outputs can be achieved. The shadow price is an indication of how difficult it would be to move a constraint on production by buying a new machine, or hiring more staff, for example. I shall return to shadow prices in more detail later.

It is common in linear programming analysis to use a term called the 'objective function'. This is a measure which the analyst seeks to maximise or minimise by adjusting the mixture of inputs and outputs. Most commonly the objective function would be something such as profit.

Since the word 'objective' has a number of overtones in the context of transferring techniques from the physical sciences to the social sciences it is important to note that the word 'objective' in this context is taken in the meaning of an aim or a goal, not as the opposite of subjective. The objective function is a target which is to be raised as far possible by adjusting the use of resources in processes.

However, I deliberately avoid using the objective function in the analysis which I offer of educational systems. The reason that I choose to avoid the objective function is that it re-introduces the idea that there is one best way of acting in a particular situation. I want rather to emphasise the range of possible actions within the constraints which are described by linear programming.

In the *Control of Education* (Lauglo & McLean, 1985) a number of authors discuss aspects of an old issue in comparative education, namely who controls education. Lauglo & McLean (1985 p. 19) argue that,

> "If the aim is to describe accurately the patterns of influence and control in education, the polarity of centralised versus decentralised control is clearly inadequate".

In this chapter I intend to examine this dichotomy of centralised/decentralised/systems and to present an approach to the control of education systems which goes beyond such a simple scheme.

Planning Decisions in a School

An example of policy control and/or influence will be given, in which techniques from linear programming are used. More work needs to be done to develop these techniques in a comparative context, but the example should make clear how a number of issues could be explored. In the example, the case of allocating funds within a school between two headings (staffing costs and materials) is considered. Who makes the decision? How much autonomy is the school permitted by the local authorities? How much change might a local interest group hope to bring about by using its influence? The answers to these questions are seldom clear-cut. Schools have autonomy within boundaries set by central authorities. In qualitative terms we can understand such a description of a single educational system. But in comparative terms, it becomes much harder to address the questions raised. Is a school in this system more tightly constrained than a school in that one? Is this school more open to pressure group influence than that one? Linear programming offers a way of providing a more detailed analysis of these questions.

Consider the case of a school allocating its financial resources between two options: staffing and material resources. This decision may be made at the local level for an individual school, or it may be made centrally for a large system of schools. It may be made consciously by a single administrator, or it may be made by default at a series of rambling staff meetings. But in any school, it must be made. Nor is it a trivial decision, as it reflects a complex response to a range of educational and pedagogic decisions; would the education of children best be served by smaller classes or by larger classes with better teaching resources, teaching machines, computer assisted instruction and so on.

The decision to allocate a particular sum of money to staffing, and another sum to material resources can be represented on a two dimensional graph, as in Figure 7.2.

(A more complex analysis is possible, further subdividing categories of expenditure: for example expenditure on material resources might be divided as between capital and recurrent expenditure. The techniques set out here can usefully be extended to more than two dimensions of policy, but for illustrative purposes it is simplest to present a two dimensional model.) The graph in Figure 7.2 shows the 'policy space' within which any school must logically lie. A point in the policy space represents a specific combination of spending on staffing and spending on material resources. For example, point A represents £400,000 spent on staffing and £100,000 spent on material resources.

Figure 7.2: A point in the policy space

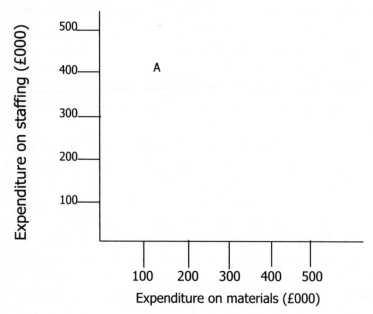

In looking at how an institution arrives at a specific point in the policy space, such as point A, it is clear that it is not the result of one individual dreaming up the figures and saying, without reference to anything else, "We shall spend £400,000 on staffing and £100,000 on material resources, and as a result we will be at point A". In any particular national setting, policy will be constrained by a number, possibly a large number, of legal, moral and political constraints.

Such constraints can be represented on the graph representing the policy space. For example, the line shown in Figure 7.3 joins all the points where the total expenditure, on staffing and material resources, adds up to £500,000. It can be seen that point A lies on it. In addition, it is clear that as the sum spent on material resources rises, so the sum spent on staffing falls, and vice versa. All the points which represents a total budget of less than £500,000 lie below the line and to the left of it; the line represents the constraint that the maximum expenditure is £500,000.

Figure 7.3: A budgetary constraint

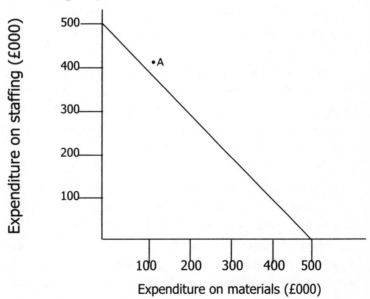

Thus, in looking at who controls the school, and how much autonomy there is at school level, we might investigate mechanisms which set such a constraint on workable policies. A legally enforceable, maximum school budget might be set directly by the national educational authorities, or the local authorities might allocate the school a budget. Indeed, both of these mechanisms might operate simultaneously, with the lower figure being the one within which the school is obliged to operate.

Using linear programming techniques necessitates a careful examination of the mechanisms which limit the freedom of choice at the school level. The issue is not simply whether there is a maximum limit to the school's expenditure, but what it is, and what elements come together to form the limit. In this way we can gain an insight, not only into who controls education, but also how it is controlled.

Similarly, we can imagine a set of elements which taken together would produce an effective constraint on the minimum amount to be spent on staffing. There may be a legally enforceable maximum student-teacher ratio, and hence a minimum number of staff to be employed in a school of a particular size. There may also be nationally set salary scales, or contracts with particular members of staff, which commit a sum of money to be spent on those teachers. The overall result of the combination of these elements is a constraint on the minimum expenditure on staffing. For the sake of argument, we might suppose this to be £300,000.

Figure 7.4 shows the line which represents an expenditure on staffing of £300,000. This line, therefore, represents the constraint discussed above. It can be seen that this minimum expenditure is independent of the spending on material resources. In a similar way, one might consider a set of elements which, together, represented a constraint on the minimum expenditure on material resources. One might imagine buildings in a specific state of dilapidation and legal requirements covering the standard of buildings in which education is conducted, which together would require that a certain minimum amount be spent on the maintenance of the buildings, and consequently on material resources. There might be other combinations of elements which would produce similar constraints. A minimum of £100,000 being spent on material resources is shown in Figure 7.5. Together, these three considerations would define a policy space within which the school could operate. Theoretically, at least, any point within those limits is attainable, as shown in Figure 7.6.

Figure 7.4: A minimum staffing budget

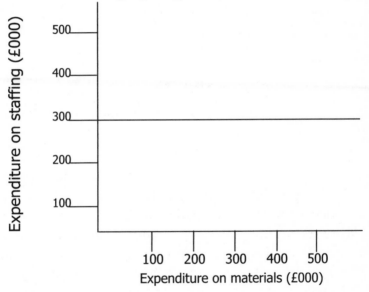

In comparative perspective, different national educational systems will leave different policy spaces available to policymakers at the school level. Civil service conditions of employment will be relevant in one country, and irrelevant in another. The technique set out here offers a descriptive tool, through which the overall pattern of national control can be brought together to show its impact upon policy at school level.

Figure 7.5: A minimum expenditure on upkeep

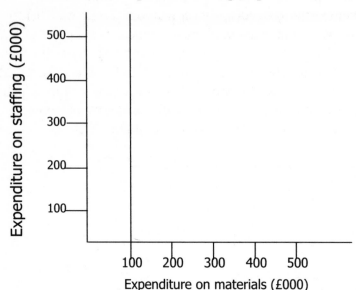

More importantly, this technique allows the impact of particular items of legislation to be evaluated. For example, there might in a system be a requirement that no class should have fewer than four pupils. If, by using this technique, it became clear that the fiscal requirements effectively amounted to a requirement that no class should have fewer than 12 pupils, the former law would be, quite obviously, irrelevant. In this way, from the mass of legislation in different fields of government which have a bearing upon education, it would be possible to identify those particular items of legislation which actually set the limits to the space in which workable policies can be found, and hence decide which policies are attainable.

Figure 7.6: Constraints and an area of attainable policies.

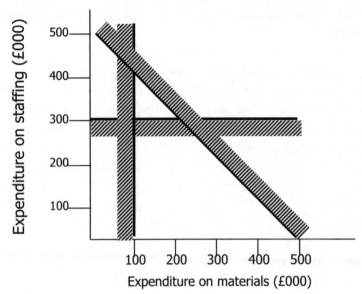

It ought not to surprise us if we discover that in some national settings there are no areas which represent attainable policies. Where a broad range of legislation has an impact on education, no thought may have been given to the ways in which these pieces of legislation produce an overall environment for educational institutions; labour law, health and safety law, local government financing legislation, transport policy, not to mention education law itself, may all have a constraining effect on educational institutions. Where these various elements have been developed separately, there is no guarantee that an educational institution would be able to satisfy all the constraints at the same time.

This situation would be represented graphically by the fact that there was no area in the policy space which was defined by the constraints as being one within which policies might work, as was the case in Figure 7.6. That is to say, schools might only be able to operate by ignoring certain legal constraints. This might make the performance of the school system especially erratic, and subject to arbitrary political changes in direction.

What one can begin to see here is that a picture of the qualitative structure of the constraints on an educational system would begin to develop. Once one starts to put a number of constraints on to the graph, one can see the importance of the central area within which the school is constrained to operate. The size of this workable area offers an indication of how tightly controlled the school is. The constraints themselves will give an indication of who controls the school. It becomes possible to evaluate whether the schools in one system are more or less tightly constrained than in another, and it becomes possible to see whether those constraints arise as a result of policy adoption at a national, regional or local level.

It would be possible to assess whether legislation which pays minute attention to detail, as in the case of the Federal Republic of Germany, is more or less constricting than legislation which is more loosely phrased, as in the case of the United Kingdom. I think that we might very well find some paradoxical results here, and there is at least the possibility that very tight legal phrasing is liberating rather than constricting. In a system of law which is put together *ad hoc*, without reference to a centralised schema, the unintended consequences of a piece of legislation may be very severe. Under the programme set out here, it would at least be possible to examine such questions.

Attainability and Sustainability

Up to this point, I have only considered those policy states which are attainable. Essentially, this is a static model of an educational system. Current policy choices, however, are affected by historic choices, and it is necessary to look at the dynamics of policy. Educational policy is not simply about what is attainable, it is also about what is sustainable.

Armitage and Smith (1972) point out that not all the policy states which are attainable can be sustained over a period of time. Certain historic decisions carry implications for the future. As a general rule, staffing costs are harder to reduce than capital expenditure, since employment contracts and terms of service generally make it difficult to reduce costs suddenly and arbitrarily in the area of staffing. In England and Wales, for example, there is the further consideration that teachers' salary scales are so ordered that, with no change in staff, staffing costs will necessarily increase year on year.

Similarly, certain items of capital expenditure may imply recurrent cost in subsequent years. The 'force' of these implied costs may be practical or legal. The purchase of a photocopying machine, for example, might not legally entail a recurrent expenditure on paper for photocopies, although in the absence of paper, the machine serves no purpose. On the other hand, entering into a leasing agreement on the same machine will involve a legal commitment to recurrent expenditure.

From any particular position in the policy space, therefore, there is a limited number of positions which can be achieved the following year. There will be some latitude for change, but in general there will be an area within which the next year's policy must lie. By making some reasonable estimates of the variables which are not legally constrained, such as probable turnover rates among staff, it will be possible to estimate the area of the policy which is attainable, year to year (see Figure 7.7). One can readily imagine circumstances in which a position which is attainable is not sustainable, which is to say, it may not be possible to remain at the same point in the policy space year after year. As an example, consider the case where deteriorating buildings require that increasing sums of money have to be spent on repairs in order to maintain premises which meet safety requirements. As time goes on this will force the institution to reduce expenditure on staffing in order to maintain the buildings, or to seek an expansion in the overall budget. (On this last issue, it should perhaps be noted that constraints are not immutable. It may be possible, by political action at an appropriate level, for participants to move or remove constraints. What is offered here is a method for analysing the constraints at any particular moment.)

There may therefore be points in the policy space which are attainable but not sustainable (see Figure 7.8). These represent inherently unstable conditions, where the institution is obliged to move over a period of time. Nor will that movement necessarily be towards parts of the policy space which offer more stable solutions.

Figure 7.7: A point which is both attainable and sustainable.

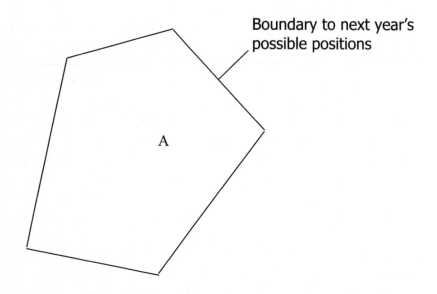

The case of the deteriorating buildings indicates the possibility that an institution can get into a condition of uncontrollable runaway.

Figure 7.8: A point which is attainable but not sustainable

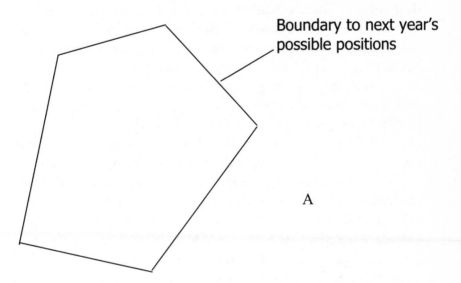

In this way it is possible to arrive at an immediately graphic description of a system of legal constraints, and their effects upon institutions. There will be those institutions for which relatively large areas of the policy space are both attainable and sustainable (Figure 7.7). Moreover, if the areas which are attainable but not sustainable tend to lead back to the sustainable areas, these will be inherently stable systems.

In contrast with these institutions, there will be others for which the sustainable areas are either small, or non-existent, and where the institutions show a marked tendency to move away from sustainable areas. These will be chronically unstable.

I now return to the question of costs which I mentioned earlier. If an institution wishes to operate outside the area of its current constraints, then in order to do so it would need to move back those boundaries in such a way as to make the desired policy position available to it. One immediate consequence of this consideration is that it emphasises that the constraints described in linear programming are not deterministic and do not ultimately settle what an institution can and cannot do. Boundaries are always movable if an institution intends to achieve a position constrained by that boundary.

However, linear programming incorporates the concept that boundaries are moved at a cost. In the engineering environment increasing capacity might involve running extra shifts or buying new machinery. In such a way the boundary could be moved but the consequences would be quite explicit.

In an educational context boundaries which constrain institutional choice can be moved but what their movement will entail will depend upon the exact nature of the constraint each boundary describes. If a boundary is set by student opinion the consequences of moving it and the cost of moving it may be quite different from those entailed in moving a boundary which is set by physical considerations.

The concept of a shadow price implies that it is perfectly reasonable for institutional policy makers to think of operating in conditions beyond the boundaries of their current constraints. However, they will also need to consider which boundaries need to be moved in order to operate in such a way and what will need to be done in order to move the boundaries.

Returning to Figure 7.6, we can see that each of the three boundaries constraining the policies of the institution can be moved. But moving them will require qualitatively different kinds of action. Increasing the overall budget of the institution will either involve persuading the budget-granting authorities to increase their subvention or it will involve independent fund-raising to give the institution an independent source of income. Reducing staffing costs may not be possible without breach of contract in the short-run but in the longer-run it may be feasible not to re-appoint for staff who retire or to replace leaving staff with younger and less experienced staff at a lower salary. In normal circumstances we would expect expenditure on materials to be the easiest boundary to move simply by cutting back on current expenditure or the repair of buildings, although the latter will also have consequences in the longer-term.

Implied in this analysis of what it takes to move a constraint is the complementary notion that working outside a boundary without moving it will have consequences which are dependent upon the nature of the constraint. Exceeding the total budget will either lead to a cumulative deficit or will lead to the directors of the institution being sued for maladministration. Reducing the expenditure on staff by breaching the contracts of employment is likely to lead to labour relation difficulties. Reducing expenditure on materials is less likely to have immediate consequences for the directors of the institution.

In general this argument can be extended to say that there are consequences of working outside the area defined by the constraints and that those consequences are fairly well defined by the nature of the boundary itself and the shadow price of moving it. Put another way, there is a family of sociological laws which state that if an institution moves beyond a constraint or boundary then certain specific consequences follow as a result of crossing a boundary. It should be noted that this is a sociological law in the way in which I understand the term 'scientific law', but that this sense is entirely divorced from any overtone of determinism. An institution can work beyond a constraint or boundary. That boundary may be moved at a cost but failure to move it while still working beyond it will have very specific and tangible consequences.

Comparative studies of different national systems of education using the techniques outlined here are well suited to answer a range of questions. Primarily, there is the question of which features of a system of constraints promote stability. In this sense, it should be noted, stability is a system analytic concept linked to controllability. This concept of stability is not necessarily linked to a political notion of stability, or adherence to the *status quo*. Certainly, a controllable system may be kept in one position by politically conservative agents, but it may also be moved in a chosen direction by political radicals. A controllable system is more likely to end up in the position which policymakers desire, whatever that is, than an unstable system. In the unstable system, undesirable side effects of policy are likely to be more prominent.

In comparative studies, however, the techniques outlined here offer further opportunities. As in the example presented here, they permit the examination of the constraints on local policymakers, and by implication the exploration of the locus and nature of control in different educational systems.

Comparative studies along these lines address not only the position of educational institutions as they now are, but also the possible positions which they could occupy without a change of constraints. The example presented here is therefore a prototype for comparative policy studies, and a method which can be used to describe national and regional settings in which specific policies can be expected to work. And, as the discussion of controllability above indicated, such studies would lead into the study of the unanticipated consequences of policies in particular circumstances.

The range of issues which can be explored using the approach set out here includes a number of topics which have been of perennial importance to comparative educationists. Their study is, consequently, of interest in its own right. It becomes indispensable, however, when one moves from the academic study of comparative education to the practical issues of international co-operation and harmonisation.

If we look at measures to harmonise certain aspects of educational institutions across national systems, such an analysis should facilitate an assessment of likely future developments. For example, if we superimpose the areas of sustainable policy for two national systems on to one graph, then it will immediately be clear whether standardisation is possible (if there are sustainable areas in common), and if not, precisely what would need to be changed in order to make them compatible. This might also reveal a number of 'hidden' features of the educational systems; if two systems are compatible, but in fact operate differently, one might well ask what makes them different, and this might in turn lead to an improved understanding of the unspoken assumptions of the two systems.

The argument presented in this chapter is that policy choices can be represented within a 'policy space' in graphical terms. Constraints on choice can be represented as areas of the policy space where policies would be expected to work. These might be translated into 'sociological laws', of the form, "If this boundary is crossed, then certain consequences for policy will follow".

In addition to describing areas where policies would not be expected to work, linear programming introduces the idea that boundaries can be moved. Again, moving boundaries will imply specific consequences.

One can thus visualise an institution or individual responding to the policy environment created for them by others. These decisions are not determined by the boundaries. But we might represent the individual as constrained within a tiny space with elastic walls, or within a larger space with rigid walls. Both the size of the workable policy space and the rigidity of the walls are important for understanding the case which is being examined.

Up to this point, I have described linear programming as a technique which can be applied when the 'rules' that restrict the policy space that is available or accessible to institutions are well defined and open to public scrutiny. From this understanding of the boundary constraints, the implications for individual institutions can be inferred. However, the inverse approach is also used, and should perhaps be mentioned, even though I do not intend to develop it fully. In a variation of linear programming that is particularly useful where the policy issues are less clear, individual institutions can be plotted onto the policy space. From the way in which they cluster, it is possible to infer where the boundaries to successful policy are. As a general rule, in such a scatter plot, most of the individual institutions occupy a central area of the policy space. Some distinctive institutions, or outliers, define an implicit boundary or envelope, within which all other institutions can be found. The identification of that envelope provides the name for this approach to linear programming – data envelope analysis.

Data envelope analysis is essentially a benchmarking technique for comparing each institution to the implicit constraint upon their activities. It raises the question, if some institutions can gain an advantage by working at the edge of what is possible, why not others? As will be apparent from the previous discussion on linear programming, any such technique, and this obviously includes data envelope analysis, can handle a range of policy dimensions. Consequently, data envelope analysis offers a technique which is at once more sensitive to institutional differences and more practically applicable than the production of over-simplified league tables based upon a crude summation of various indicators.

The beauty of using linear programming in the ways described in this chapter is that large amounts of complex data can be incorporated into an understanding. The result will reflect the complexity without unnecessary over-simplification, but should provide a relatively straightforward account of the policy issues concerned. It should be clear that such models provide a basis for developing theory which directly addresses the concerns of policy makers and practitioners. If we wish to move an institution from its current position and mode of operation to a new place within the policy space, the practical implications for policy will be clear. This approach serves to highlight the shortcomings of current theory and may go some way to explain why policy makers have difficulty engaging with research findings.

In the next chapter I develop a linear programming model of a specific set of financial constraints as they applied to polytechnics in a particular historic period. For readers who wish to skip over the mathematics involved, that chapter can be ignored. However, it is presented as an example of how such policy related studies can be developed.

CHAPTER EIGHT: LINEAR PROGRAMMING AND EDUCATIONAL POLICY

One of the areas where implicit theory has been rife has been in that area of educational policy making and creating a policy environment. The implicit theory here has been that if central authorities or government makes resources available for an educational development then that educational development will be taken up in an uncomplicated way.

In this chapter I will examine the policy environment for higher education which was created in the UK between 1988 and 1994 and particularly in 1992/93. In 1988 a group of institutions which had been under local government control, the Polytechnics, were established as independent foundations, funded by the newly established Polytechnic and Colleges Funding Council (PCFC). This body thought that it had a direct hand on 'the levers of policy' which it would be able to operate by adjusting the financial parameters controlling resources available to higher education. In fact it was the case that by providing an appropriate economic environment it was possible for the PCFC to steer polytechnics towards expansion and growth in student numbers. What followed in the subsequent period was an attempt to adapt the mechanisms which had been put in place to encourage the system to follow other goals than simple expansion, such as improved quality. One of the conclusions which one is bound to draw is that the operation of those policy levers was poorly understood and that it was not in fact a simple matter to divert the whole system towards those goals which latterly became part of government policy. The experiment was ended with draconian measures to cap student numbers when it became apparent that financial levers were not effective in reducing the rate of growth of institutions. Exactly how those policy levers operated is shown in the following study which uses techniques from linear programming to describe the planning environment in which institutions found themselves.

Funding for higher education institutions in Britain comes from a variety of sources. The largest single funder for most institutions is the funding council, channelling government funds to institutions. Between 1988 and 1993, the universities were funded by the Universities Funding Council (UFC), and the polytechnics and colleges were funded by the PCFC. The PCFC developed innovative funding mechanisms, including the use of 'bidding' by institutions both for student numbers and the funds associated with them.

The second major source of institutions' funds was student fees. In the late 1980s these were increased to reflect Government policy, and to make institutions more responsive to 'market' pressures. The interaction of the two main sources of funds was complicated because institutions tended to recruit students beyond those funded by the funding councils, relying on the fee income alone. The raising of fee levels enhanced the value of those 'fee only' students. In the PCFC sector, institutions had the further incentive that the bidding process offered a way of increasing the number of PCFC funded students.

A Rule Governed Funding System

Through the bidding and recruiting process, institutions tried to secure their position with regard to overall funding and student numbers. This can be represented on a two dimensional policy space, with the axes representing student numbers and total funding (Figure 8.1). An institution with 10,000 students and a unit of resource of £3,000 per head (and consequently an overall budget of £30 million) would therefore be at point A in the policy space.

Figure 8.1: Recruitment Policy Space

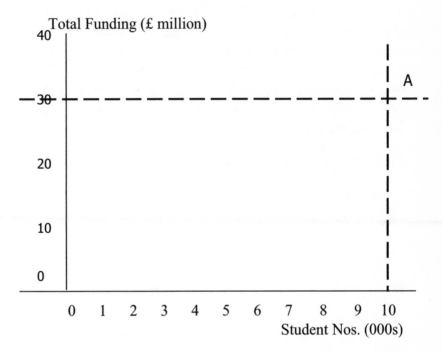

The year-on-year impact of bidding and recruiting under different rules can then be evaluated. For the purposes of illustration, I will assume that the 1992-93 rules are in operation, which means that the starting point for calculations was the student numbers and funding in 1991-92, shown in Figure 8.1. The subsequent year's position, or rather the range of positions at which the institution at point A could arrive by judicious use of the instruments of policy available to it, can be calculated by following the steps below.

The first step is to calculate the point, A_1, by taking 90 per cent of the previous student numbers and 90 per cent of the previous funding, as shown in Figure 8.2. This was the base from which an institution started, either bidding for students and funding from PCFC, or recruiting fee-only students. In graphical terms, A_1 is found by drawing a line from A to the origin of the graph, and moving one tenth of the way towards the origin (Figure 8.2). In effect, this point is the lower left hand corner of the polygon which bounds the positions which institution A can elect to be in. This is the case because it is hard to imagine an institution choosing to engineer its own contraction beyond this point, although poor recruiting could conceivably have this effect. The institution could then select a position within the policy space by applying one of two policies recruiting fee-only students or recruiting bid-supported students.

Figure 8.2: The lower boundary of the policy space

Total Funding
(£million)

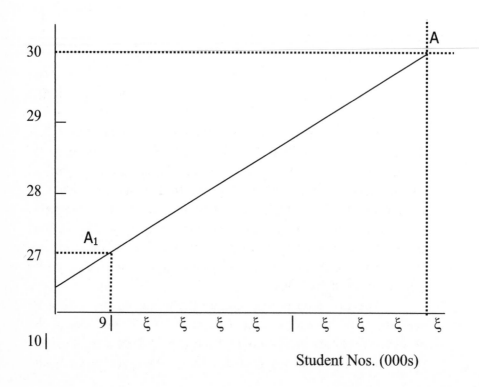

Student Nos. (000s)

Since fee-only students are the simpler case, I will deal with that first. If the fees were £1,675 (as they were in 1992-93) there is a line through A_1 with a slope of £1,675 per student, along which the institution could move by recruiting more or fewer fee-only students (the heavy line in Figure 8.2). An additional 1,000 fee-only students add £1.675 million to the institution's budget. This forms the lower boundary of the polygon which contains all the points which the institution can move to. This is the case because an institution could not take students on conditions worse than fee-only. The point of the bidding process for the institution was to attempt to improve the unit of resource above fee-only. In terms of the unit of resource, movement of the institution along this line was the worst possible case.

A similar calculation leads to a line describing all the points which can be achieved by recruiting students supported by bids for PCFC funds. However, in this case the line of opportunities is a parabola, rising to a maximum above and to the right of A_1. This conclusion comes from a consideration of the moderation process used by PCFC. This, perhaps, requires some further analysis, as it is not so intuitively obvious as the case for fee-only students.

In order to see what the best case is, and to identify the upper boundary of the policy space, we need to consider bid-funded students. That can best be understood by looking in detail at the moderation process used by PCFC in allocating bid money to institutions. The moderation process is described in detail by Pratt and Hillier (1991), and the figures used here are based on their example.

Suppose that the bids submitted by various institutions are entered on a graph like that in Figure 8.3 and that a moderation line is drawn on. This line indicates that a maximum bid of £4,000 will be paid, or that an overall increase of 40 per cent of student numbers will be granted, or some combination in between. In all cases fee income has to be added to the bid figure shown on the moderation diagram. If we plot the whole range of bid possibilities on the policy space, the resulting line is a parabola which peaks, in this case with a bid recruitment of 20 per cent, which yields a gross income of £7.35 million for an institution with 10,000 students. (This figure is for 20 per cent growth, or 2,000 students each producing £2,000 in bid-funding and £1,675 in fees.) From point A_1 to this maximum, this parabola forms the upper left section of the boundary to the space which the institution can occupy. Bid-funding of all students beyond the core represents the best attainable case in terms of the unit of resource.

Figure 8.3: A moderation line (after Pratt and Hillier)

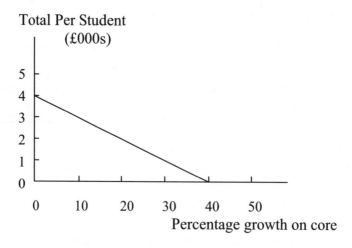

It is possible to see the impact of applying different rules to the process described here, as illustrated in Figure 8.4. Moderation was a technique applied in most of the subject areas defined by PCFC, but it was not used in all subject areas. Effectively, it was a way of distributing a total cash sum such that institutions could fund a few students at high rates, or more students at lower rates. But moderation was not employed in all subject areas. Where the number of bids was low compared to the cash allocated, moderation was not employed. Below a certain cut-off figure, institutions got everything that they bid for. If we suppose, in the example looked at here, that the cut off was £4,000, then an institution could bid for, and get, any number of students they wished. Under such a rule, an institution could move along a straight line with a slope of £4,000 per student (or £5,675 per student if one adds on the fee income). This line is in fact the tangent to the parabola at point A_1 (Figure 8.4).

Figure 8.4: The upper boundary of the policy space

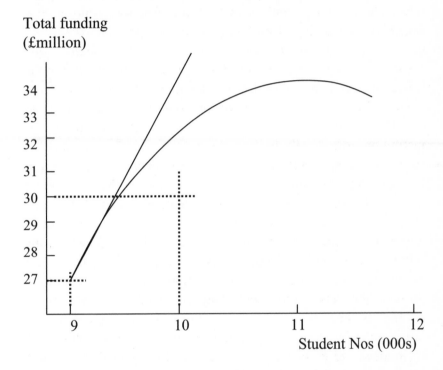

The straight line represents the condition where an institution could recruit any number of students at a fixed price. The parabola falls below this line as a result of moderation. As one moves right across the graph, the gap between the parabola and the straight line increases, which is to say that where more students were bid for, the impact of cash limits was greatest.

Other mechanisms for limiting total expenditure could be imagined, resulting in different curves. But the important point is that the straight line was only used where PCFC was not concerned to limit expenditure. One cannot, therefore, imagine an institution moving up indefinitely along this line; at some point funding would have to be limited.

Returning to the case where moderation was applied, we have two policies which the institution can use to move from A_1, and two lines which describe the points which can be arrived at using those policies. These are a straight line of slope £1,675 per student, representing fee only students, and a parabola rising to a peak where 20 per cent growth is bid for, representing bid-funded students. By combining these two policies, recruiting bid-funded and recruiting fee-only funded students, the institution can extend the polygon of possible positions for the subsequent year between the parallel lines of slope £1,675 per student (Figure 8.5). There is no obvious limit to the extent to which this polygon can be extended. For any particular institution, there will be a limit to the absolute number of students, set by its accommodation. There may also be a limit to the percentage growth which can occur through the recruitment of fee-only students. The precise mechanism through which the latter might occur would need further consideration, but it might, for example, take time for an institution to adapt to the implied reduction in the unit of resource. In 1992-93 there were no formal rules which limited the expansion of an institution through fee-only recruitment. But an institution planning to double its size by fee-only recruitment might have attracted unwelcome attention which might have affected its reputation, or induced the PCFC to reconsider its attitude in this area and introduce formal rules.

Figure 8.5: Attainable policies

Total Funding
(£million)

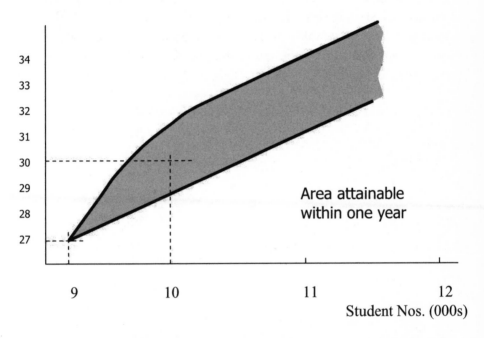

Student Nos. (000s)

It should be noted that, although the polygon thus arrived at marked the absolute limit of movement from one year to the next, not all places in the polygon are equally available. An institution could move at will along the lower, fees-only, boundary. Moving at or near the upper boundary requires perfect anticipation of the bidding process, and was consequently less likely, though not impossible.

Impact of the Rules on Different Institutions

The next step in developing an overview of the impact of bidding on institutions is to generalise the insight gained to a range of institutions. Since all calculations used refer to percentage increases, the conclusions can easily be extended to all institutions of the same size. If we take three institutions A, B and C, all with 10,000 students, but with different historic levels of funding, this can be seen quite clearly (Figure 8.6). The first calculation of 90 per cent core funding for 90 per cent of core students, involves each institution moving towards the origin to points A_1, B_1, and C_1. But the reasoning for the shape of the polygon of attainable policies is identical for all three institutions. Consequently, the shape and size of the polygon is identical for the three institutions (Figure 8.6).

Figure 8.6: Comparison of institutions of the same size

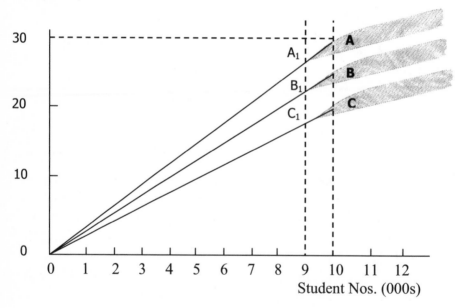

A comparison of the three cases makes a number of things apparent. The original positions of the three institutions all lie within their polygon of possibilities. That is to say, all three could, if they chose, continue exactly as they were; their positions were sustainable. However, they were differently placed in relation to those polygons. Institution A is higher in its polygon than either B or C. Consequently, institution A would find it harder to sustain its position. On the other hand, before one wastes too much sympathy on institution A, it can also be clearly seen that A's position was quite unattainable for institution C, at least in the short-term.

It can also be seen that by moving up above point A, or down below point C, a condition will be reached where an institution's original position did not lie within the polygon of possible positions for the next year. In this case the institution was in a position which was not sustainable. There are two obvious ways in which this could happen, but only one of them is likely to be of any practical consequence. In the first place the institution might be working on a unit of resource lower than £1,675 per student. In that case, its position would be bound to improve, even if it only recruited more fee-only students.

Secondly and more importantly, an institution might be unable to sustain its position because its unit of resource was too high. It is important to establish what 'too high' would mean in this context. The initial calculation of funding involved a 10 per cent cut in student numbers and funding. This was indicated graphically as the move from A to A_1. In order to maintain its position, any institution would have to recoup both the student numbers and the funding. For an institution at the highest sustainable unit of resource as much as possible of this funding would have be secured with bid supported students. This might be described as a 'cash recovery' policy, where an institution simply used the bidding process to recover the core funding and core students which are 'lost' in the first stage of the funding calculation.

The calculation is facilitated by taking a sample institution of 10,000. Its core will be 9,000 students, and a cash recovery policy will involve bidding for 1000 students. Using the moderation line from the example above, greatest income achievable for each of these students is £3,000 bid, plus £1,675 fees, or a total income of just under £4.7 million for 1,000 students. An institution with a student population of 10,000, and a total budget of £47 million or less will be able to pursue a cash recovery policy; one with a greater budget will not.

One striking feature of this exercise is the very different figure which we arrive at for the maximum sustainable unit of resource, compared with the first impression one gains from Figure 8.3 showing the moderation line. In this example, the moderation line shows PCFC prepared to fund students at a maximum bid price of £4,000. If we add fees, this gives funding of £5,675. But by definition, very few students can be funded at this level. When we gross this up across the whole institution, it is clear that the highest sustainable unit of resource is something under £4,700 per head, substantially less than the amount of money one might have concluded from the moderation line. And, as has been noted, even this figure is only available to institutions doing extremely well in the bidding process.

Naturally, the shape of the parabola which an institution can follow using the bidding process, and consequently the maximum sustainable unit of resource, is affected by the moderation line used. For example, if a maximum bid of £4,000, or a maximum growth of 30 per cent were used, instead of the 40 per cent above, then the maximum sustainable unit of resource would drop to £4,350 per student. A similar drop results from reducing the maximum bid price to £3,600 while leaving maximum growth at 40 per cent.

Now, if we take these results and generalise them for institutions operating on the same rules year after year, we can conclude that two lines mark the boundaries of sustainable existence. These are lines indicating £1,675 per student, and £4,700 per student (Figure 8.7). The right-hand of this policy area is likely to be bounded by conditions which are specific to an institution, such as historic recruitment from a region, or facilities.

But although all points within these boundaries are sustainable, they are not all attainable. As has been seen earlier, an institution cannot move at will upwards and to the left. At any specific point in the policy space, (Figure 8.7) there is a restriction by a line of £4,700 per student which prevents an institution moving any closer to the upper limit of the sustainable policy space.

Figure 8.7: Area of sustainable policy

Total Funding
(£million)

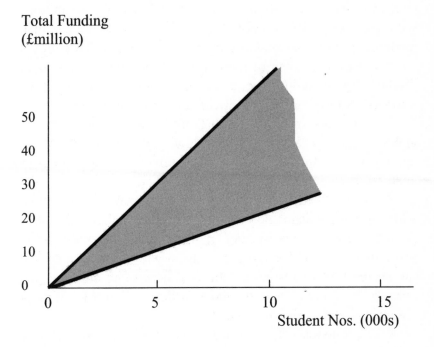

Student Nos. (000s)

The policy space described here, therefore, does not produce a playing field which can in any sense be described as level. In the first place, there is a universally felt slope towards lower units of resource which pushes all institutions towards the lower right section. Clever manipulation of the bidding system can, at best, postpone drift in this direction. The long term indicates a move in this direction. This will hardly surprise anyone as this appears to be the point and purpose of the policy.

On the other hand, and perhaps more surprisingly, institutions with historically high units of resource have a distinct advantage, in the sense that they can attain positions which are not available to other institutions. Being on the very upper limit of the sustainable policy space is, of course, to be sitting on a greasy pole, and movement towards lower units of resource are almost inevitable. However, institutions which have high costs can at least attain these positions, and have the option to try and sustain them, or at worst to slow to a minimum the drift towards a more even distribution of funding. Institutions with high units of resource can *sustain* higher levels than institutions with low units of resource can *attain*. This means that an historic element of funding is still present in the current funding system, and it is not at all clear that this element will be removed by the year-on-year effect of the bidding system.

We might now try turning the insights gained around, and ask questions about how this should inform an institution's approach to the bidding process. Most obviously, the process of analysis considered here gives very specific answers to the question of whether an institution is sustainable. Institutions which are not sustainable will have to follow policies designed to increase their stability. For all institutions, but particularly institutions with higher costs, expansion will normally lead to a fall in the unit of resource. One could therefore suppose that cheaper institutions will be those which will most willingly embrace a policy of expansion.

Institutions with historically high unit costs may choose simply to maintain their position through a policy of 'cash recovery', by which they use the bidding system to recover the ten per cent funding removed by PCFC. For institutions with high unit costs, the only way to improve the unit of resource may be to suffer a, possibly temporary, reduction in size.

Overall, then, the analysis suggests that the bidding process was likely to promote an expansion of historically cheap institutions, and stagnation, or possibly even a contraction, among historically expensive institutions. While this would appear to have been in line with an overall national policy of increasing higher education provision with increasing cost efficiency, it raises questions about quality, and in precisely which sectors growth should be stimulated.

If we consider an institution which is attempting to secure stability through a cash replacement policy, the analysis offers some interesting conclusions. At the beginning of the bidding round, the institution was at C, a sustainable policy position, as illustrated in Figure 8.9. We suppose that it is institutional policy to maintain the institution at that point. The core funding is represented by the calculation of C_1, a ten per cent reduction of students and funding. In order to return to point C, the bidding process must result in the institution arriving at point P, after which movement to C can be secured by recruiting fee-only students.

We might therefore anticipate a tendency towards bids in the area of P, or even Q, which represents a higher unit of resource than P. Looking at the historic outcomes of the moderation process, a reasonable attempt could be made to estimate the range P to Q, and we might therefore expect more and more institutions to aim to put in bids in that range. In short, far from stimulating institutions to undercut each other in the bidding process, the overall logic of the moderation process would appear to produce a pressure towards slightly above average bid prices.

More importantly, for an institution wishing to maintain its position, anywhere on the arc PQ would be effective. So long as the institution is not too close to the boundary of the sustainable policy area (i.e. so long as the institution does not have high unit costs), success can be achieved over a fairly large range of bid prices. Institutional success in the bidding process is only critically dependent upon bid prices if the institution is trying to maintain a historically high unit cost.

All of this suggests that an institution would be expected to place an above average bid for as many students as it thinks it could reasonably recruit, and adjust its recruitment to match its overall policy by the addition of fee-only students after the outcome of the bidding process is known. All of this should be relatively easy to achieve, so long as there was a reasonable degree of stability in the moderation process. In the absence of this condition, consistent planning over the bidding and recruitment process would appear to be impossible anyway.

Figure 8.8: Bidding for "cash recovery"

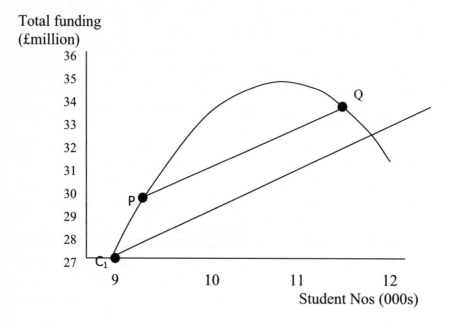

Total funding
(£million)

Student Nos (000s)

Overall Policy Objectives and Policy Instruments

There are some interesting aspects to this case study of national funding policy. The overall policy of the PCFC was to provide the maximum number of places at the minimum cost, providing for certain safeguards on quality. It can be seen that this is a macro-effect of the policy which was adopted. The corresponding assumption, that this would lead to high price competitiveness among institutions in the same sector, is not necessarily linked to expansion of the system. Even the formation of an informal cartel, setting minimum bid prices, would not necessarily frustrate the overall policy objective.

This overall mismatch between assumptions about the link between national and institutional policies is more apparent in certain areas. Although there was overall national pressure for the expansion of student numbers, this was not felt equally by institutions. Traditionally expensive institutions could only maintain their historic positions by remaining at the same size, while traditionally cheap institutions had everything to gain from expansion. It is not clear whether this was in line with national policy. There are several ways in which national expansion could be achieved. One is through the stimulation of cheap institutions, another is through stimulating the increased efficiency of expensive institutions. In national terms these policies might be financially equivalent. However, if the expensive institutions also had a history of quality which one wished to impart to the whole sector, the expansion of expensive institutions, linked to increased cost efficiency, would be a desirable goal. National policy did not appear to encourage expansion through this route in the early 1990s.

The analysis which I have offered here, as an example of the application of linear programming, was one that I first developed in the early 1990s. It was followed by a similar analysis of the funding mechanism which was put in place by the Higher Education Funding Council for England (HEFCE) after 1994. A number of general observations about national policy can be drawn from these analyses.

The Funding Councils in the United Kingdom believed that by operating an open system for calculating funds they would be able to steer institutions in directions which were desirable for national policy. This was not a view that was restricted to the United Kingdom but which found expression in many national systems of funding higher education across Europe. The basic assumption was that Funding Councils at a national level had available to them a number of policy levers and that by adjusting the various parameters in the funding system, by tweaking the levers of national policy, institutions could be steered in a direction which was desirable. Even in the analysis of the PCFC funding mechanisms a number of portents of the future could be seen. Most importantly, it is clear that the linkage between particular policy levers and outcomes was not as simple as was imagined by the Funding Council itself.

Even though the same mechanisms were applied to all institutions the national framework did not produce a level playing field. The funding provisions had a differential effect depending upon the historic level of funding of the institution considered. The funding mechanism was extremely successful in promoting expansion – which was one of the major goals of national policy – but, as the analysis has made clear, the pressure towards expansion was not felt equally by all institutions.

Another feature of the analysis which was to have great importance but which was not necessarily obvious at the time was that the areas of attainability which institutions had available to them were not bounded on the upper right-hand side. This shows in detailed terms that the funding mechanisms had not made provision for limiting the expansion of institutions. It was not thought that excessive expansion was going to be a major problem. However, the push towards expansion was so successful that it subsequently became clear that government policy would need to address controlling the rate of expansion.

By the mid 1990s institutions were expanding so rapidly that, although the unit of resource per student was falling, the overall budget for higher education was increasing as institutions expanded. The government felt the need at this point to limit expansion in order to meet their overall fiscal targets.

The theory which had been set out in the early 1990s suggested that the funding councils had a range of policy levers which they could adjust in order to steer the national system of higher education in any direction that they chose. Consequently in the mid 1990s they tried to adjust the parameters of the funding mechanism to choke off excessive expansion. At that point it became clear that the levers to slow expansion were not working. A mechanism which had been designed in the first place to promote expansion had not, as it came to appear in the mid 1990s, been fitted with a brake. In the end the government took measures outside the funding mechanisms in order to impose limits to expansion while imposing penalties on institutions which expanded more rapidly than intended.

The funding of teaching which has been analysed in this example using linear programming was not the only funding mechanism through which national policy was expressed for institutions. Similar transparent formula funding was being used to allocate research funds. Some of the pressures on institutions from the funding mechanisms for research were similar to those from the funding mechanisms for teaching. In both cases, funding formulae which were applied uniformly to all institutions had the effect of stimulating differentiation between institutions. One conclusion, and it is a conclusion that arises very clearly from this analysis, is that applying the same rules to all institutions does not necessarily produce a level playing field.

At least since the time of Kandel (1954), it has been common to analyse educational systems in terms of whether they are centralised or decentralised. This is particularly true of studies in a comparative context. The linear programming analysis suggests that the relationship between central and local authorities can be handled in a much more sensitive and a much more instructive way. Central authorities set general parameters within which local authorities work. Central authorities set a legal and financial and policy framework which sets boundaries for the decision-making processes at a regional or local level.

Using a linear programming analysis it is no longer necessary to polarise systems as centralised or decentralised, as though all power resided in a single location, but the interaction of decisions made at a national, local, institutional or even departmental level can be studied in some detail. Such studies are made rather simpler by the growing use of transparent systems of allocating funding, as in the case of the PCFC funding mechanism.

One of the most pervasive beliefs in terms of policy making is that resources and funding can be used to steer institutions and individuals towards directions of national policy. What the study of linear programming demonstrates is that the link between resources and general policy is frequently much more complicated than is commonly assumed. Linear programming provides a tool with which one can examine how effective specific regulations are in terms of producing a general direction of policy steer. What is more, individual changes to parts of the funding allocation can be investigated to see what effect that will have on the range of policies available to institutions and individuals. In this way, the link between the detail of funding mechanisms and overall policy direction can be examined critically. In addition, judgements can be made about how robust the mechanisms are for producing particular outcomes. By making clear the links between details of regulation and overall policy steer, such analysis provides useful tools for developing better policy.

CHAPTER NINE: GROUP DECISION MAKING

Linear programming and two-person game theory are necessarily the simplest of the models which are available from operational research and which can be applied to Educational Studies. While they incorporate the non-causal aspects, dictated by the moral constraints which I regard as important, they are very abstract from actual situations in which education is conducted. The main consideration in examining linear programming and two person game theory has been to show that we can develop an understanding of how individual agents can make decisions which are adapted to their setting without being determined by it. These techniques allow us to study individual actions within a relatively autonomous framework, without falling into the trap which Archer describes as upward conflation.

In order to maintain relative autonomy without falling into the trap of downward conflation, we need to recognise that they way in which the choices of individuals interact, and add together to form an overall planning environment are complex and may occasionally be counter-intuitive.

Multi-person game theory can help us model specific incidents in educational life which involve groups of individuals expressing preferences through voting, as might happen in staff meetings, governing bodies, academic boards and so on, or less formally in classroom settings. These issues are explored, in relation to group decisions in education, in this chapter.

A Model Classroom

I noticed that when I was a classroom teacher in schools, I frequently presided over a classroom where most of the children were working conscientiously, while a group of three or four boys (generally) were misbehaving and being disruptive. I offer a game theory account of how this happened.

Figure 9.1: A Multi-Person Game of Classroom Discipline

Level of 'Reward'

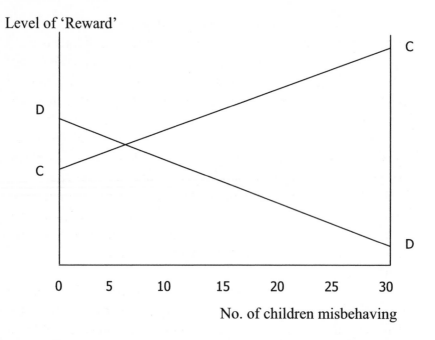

No. of children misbehaving

Line DD represents the benefits to a child who misbehaves: suppose that an increase in my attention might conceivably be a benefit as might be the status gained from being a rebel or simply having more fun. As more children misbehave (moving right on the graph) the benefits which are available to those who misbehave decrease.

Line CC represents the benefits to a child who behaves; that benefit might be improved marks, better understanding or other rewards. Those rewards increase as more children misbehave, as there are fewer people to share the approval.

If we consider that the class is well behaved, with no child misbehaving (extreme left of diagram), then the line DD is higher than the line CC, and one child who decides to misbehave (move from benefit line CC to line DD) will be 'better off'. One child is now misbehaving. There is still an advantage to the second child who chooses to misbehave (although the benefit is slightly reduced). This logic continues until about five children are misbehaving, at which point line DD crosses below line CC, and there is no advantage for a behaving child to misbehave.

If we start form the other end, with thirty children misbehaving, and me distraught in a corner, there is an incentive for the first child to decide to behave, and gain the benefits of approval (moving from benefit line DD to CC). Similarly for the second, third, fourth and fifth child, although every time the benefit reduces slightly. Order is gradually restored to the classroom, until twenty five children are behaving, when the line CC crosses below line DD, and there is no incentive for the last five to behave.

My classroom has an equilibrium with twenty five children working conscientiously, and five misbehaving. Notice, however, that this tells me nothing about which children will misbehave. I might take one of my regular trouble makers to one side, give him a good talking to, and suggest the advantages of him behaving better. At the next lesson he arrives, eager to learn, and puts himself conscientiously to study. It is to no avail; another trouble maker will be created in his stead, taking advantage of the fact that only four children are misbehaving, and a fifth can gain benefits by joining them.

With hindsight, this seems to me to have been an all too common feature of my classroom management. I can begin to understand it in terms of the rewards and punishments I structured into classroom settings. Other colleagues, I noted, could arrange their classrooms differently, some with all thirty children rioting, others with thirty children studiously working in their desks. I have to wonder whether I set out more or less deliberately to have the classrooms that I had, since I was never quite comfortable in either a riot or a silent classroom.

That is by the by. Let me simply reiterate that this is a model of educational theory in several senses; it is explicit, it is clearly elaborated; it says nothing about the behaviour of individuals, and it has general explanatory power in terms of understanding different classroom settings (by arranging lines CC and DD differently). The behaviour of individuals is not determined by their genetic make-up, nor by their socialisation. They act as free agents in accord with the 'logic of the situation'. But it should also be noted that the pattern of group behaviour is not exactly the outcome of any one individual's choices; there is partial autonomy between individual and group.

Earlier in this volume I have looked at two person zero sum games and particularly games against nature as a way of describing educational choices. I have looked at two person non zero sum games or co-operative games as a way of gaining insight into such phenomena as the behaviour of twins, or other questions of choice where the identity of participants may be confused by observers. In the example that started this chapter, I have looked at multi-person zero sum games as a way of describing and gaining insights into group situations such as classroom discipline. All of these game theory models share a common theme which is the partial autonomy between different levels of understanding, the social group and the individual. Since this is a feature of game theory models and is important to our understanding and describing of ethical agents, then it makes sense to ask whether game theory has any other models to offer. The obvious framework is that of multi-person, non zero sum games or multi-person co-operative games. These deal with areas of coalition formation and decision making in groups such as one might find in committees or less formal groups which try to arrive at policy decisions for the whole group. Since committees are so ubiquitous in formal organisations such as schools, colleges and universities the thought suggests itself that this may also be a fruitful tool for examining educational processes. As one would expect, such models of group choice also offer a partial autonomy between group choices and individual choices.

Arrow's Impossibility Theorem

The key to understanding this autonomy is that group choices run across probably the most important result in game theory, namely Arrow's Impossibility Theorem. Suppose that we have a group of three people who have to make a choice and who have set patterns of individual preference. For example, suppose that three people group together to buy a bottle of wine and their preferences are shown in Figure 9.1. The meaning of the matrix is that participant A would prefer to have a bottle of red wine. His or her second choice would be a bottle of white wine and his or her third choice would be a bottle of rosé wine. Participant B has preferences which run in the order, a bottle of rosé wine is preferable to a bottle of red wine is preferable to a bottle of white wine. Participant C has a preference for white wine over rosé wine over red wine.

Figure 9.2: Preferences in a Group of Three People

	First	Second	Third
Preference of A	Red	White	Rosé
Preference of B	Rosé	Red	White
Preference of C	White	Rosé	Red

This indecisive group has a bottle of red wine on the table. Before they open it they have to decide whether that is indeed the bottle of wine they are going to choose or whether they would vote for a different bottle of wine. One can see that on a majority vote of two to one the group will choose to exchange the bottle of red wine for a bottle of rosé wine. Once the bottle of rosé wine is on the table a majority of two to one would prefer a bottle of white wine over the bottle of rosé wine. And once the bottle of white wine is on the table a majority of two to one would prefer a bottle of red wine to a bottle of white wine. This is Condorcet's paradox; it suggests that a group of three people need not necessarily have a clear-cut preference even though each individual has a well-ordered and well-defined preference for the choices which are to be made. The partial autonomy of group decision relative to the individual decisions can be seen in the fact that for an individual, we would expect preferences to be transitive. That is to say if I prefer a bottle of rosé wine to a bottle of white wine and I prefer a bottle of white to a bottle of red wine it is reasonable to expect that I would prefer a bottle of red wine to a bottle of rosé wine. It is not reasonable to expect a group decision to be transitive in this same way and the indecisive group of three people will never open the bottle of wine because they are perpetually able to see a better group choice than any bottle which stands on the table.

This intractable problem over choosing a bottle of wine has the name Condorcet's paradox. The paradox is generalised in Arrow's impossibility theorem which states that there is no way of making group choices which can meet a number of simple criteria. According to Arrow an ideal mechanism for aggregating individual choices to make a group choice would:

> Always produce a definitive answer.
> Be independent of irrelevant criteria.
> Not be dictated by a single individual or small group.
> Be Pareto optimal.
> (Colman, 1982)

These various conditions perhaps need some explanation. The notion that the method of aggregating individual choices should always produce a definitive answer and not be a dictatorship are self-explanatory. If our group of drinkers were prepared always to rely on the choice of A then there would be no difficulty in selecting a bottle of wine – it would be red. However, in the example described above the drinkers were relying on majority voting and that system of majority voting did not produce a definitive solution.

The condition that the method of aggregating preferences should be independent of irrelevant options suggests that preferences should only relate to the colour of the wine and not, for example, to the colour of the wallpaper. The last condition, of Pareto optimality, simply states that if any one of the participants changes their order of preferences then the group decision should be likely to move in the same direction as the choice made by the individual. For example if participant C were to say, "No I have changed my mind and prefer rosé wine to white wine", then it should not be the case that the group choice should be white wine since C's preferences have moved towards rosé.

What Arrow's impossibility theorem suggests, and the example above of class discipline emphasises, is that group choices have an independent existence which is not easily derived from knowing about the individual preferences. Once again, the partial autonomy of group decisions from individual decisions is at issue here.

Areas where group decisions have to be made about policy which involves a number of different criteria are relatively common in education. For example the university or school must decide where to position itself to attract students. This will involve a committee, probably a board of governors or an academic board, deciding whether they are to place emphasis in particular subject areas to promote their quality as a teaching institution or as an agency which develops social skills and so on. The institution must prioritise the way it sells itself to prospective students.

At first sight, the most directly applicable theoretical framework in this field is by Gradstein and Nitzan (1989) on the strategies to be adopted by individuals or bodies competing for 'rents', or benefits which exceed the limited resources which they have to bid for them. Gradstein and Nitzan argue that this framework is directly applicable to companies bidding for contracts, and would therefore appear to apply to institutions bidding for students. However, the restrictions which they have to introduce to develop the theoretical position are so limiting as to bring the analogy into question. All bidders are supposed to have equal resources, and it is supposed that a contract will be secured by the individual or group which devotes most resources to the tender.

This leads to the intuitively attractive conclusion that universities and schools do better to concentrate all their resources in the areas where they are strongest. This would suggest a progressive specialisation in subject areas, as institutions focus their profiles year after year. But at an equally intuitive level, it is not clear that the resources applied to developing a tender within a university, college or school can be used in this way. Within an institution, it is not obvious that expertise can be transferred from engineering, and successfully utilised in fine arts. And between institutions, it is not clear that all resources are qualitatively the same, and that equal amounts of effort within two competing institutions will produce equal likelihood of attracting students. In general terms, therefore, Gradstein and Nitzan's analysis, and its conclusion that institutions should put all of their eggs in one basket, would not appear to be applicable.

Much of the theoretical interest in the area of group decision making has focussed upon the activity of political parties and the way in which they should position themselves in order to attract voters. If we think of political parties as arranging themselves along a spectrum from left to right then political parties should position themselves where they can attract most voters. Where only one criterion of left or right is involved this leads to the conclusion that the party should locate itself in the position of the median voter. This is supposed to explain why political parties have a tendency towards occupying the central ground and becoming more similar to each other since extreme parties can only attract relatively small numbers of voters. This might be analogous to institutions positioning themselves along a spectrum from research orientated institutions to teaching orientated institutions. According to the median voter theorem institutions should position themselves mid-way along the spectrum where they will be able to attract the largest number of prospective students.

Early work on voting behaviour led to the development of the 'median voter theorem'. If we suppose that institutions are judged on a single criterion, and that each prospective student has an identifiable opinion about where their ideal institution should lie on that spectrum, and that students will choose the institution nearest to their ideal on the spectrum then there is only one sensible place to submit a bid: all institutions should aim to position themselves at the preference of the median voter. Any bid to the left or right of this spectrum must attract fewer votes. (Although this result derived from consideration of only two institutions the argument broadly applied to more than two.)

The conclusion, therefore, is the rather cynical one that the process of bidding involves all institutions attempting to guess the more or less central position of student preferences, and, within the limits set by the insights of the institutions, developing identical profiles. At the very least, this would suggest a tendency towards the central position, and a tendency away from innovative positions. Similar conclusions were drawn about the tendency of political parties to move towards the centre, though there has been considerable debate over whether this drift is observable, and the results would appear to be fairly inconclusive.

The situation becomes more complicated if one takes into account the fact that groups frequently make decisions, not on a single criterion, but on a range of criteria. The theoretical perspective on this is even less rosy. Consider the case of a committee choosing to allocate resources between faculties. Even when individuals have clearly defined preferences, the committee as a whole may not, as seen above.

Initially the goal of decision theory was to generalise the one dimensional 'median voter theorem' to a policy space which has two or more dimensions. Again, it was assumed that each voter would have an ideal point, and vote for the position nearest to this. It was similarly supposed that there would be a theoretical drift towards the centre. As things turned out, the result of introducing more than one selection criterion is very different.

Unless very specific, and in most cases unrealistic, assumptions are made about the pattern of preferences of prospective students, it transpires that it is possible to select a sequence of preference votes which collectively make up a path through the policy space. Moreover, by making this path long enough, it is possible to move through almost the entire policy space. In simple terms, the committee's final choice could lie anywhere; and the final decision is open to manipulation, in the sense that through judicious selection of the order of two by two comparisons, the committee can be led to a specific conclusion.

Such a committee could in principle be steered to any policy by an all-knowing agent who knows the preferences of the committee members and could thereby secure any result which the agenda-setter wished.

This result places the study of such preference patterns more firmly in chaos theory than in decision theory. It leads to the conclusion, hardly less cynical than that produced by the 'median voter theorem', that the decision of committees are a lottery, and could be controlled by omniscient committee officers.

On the positive side, the analysis in two or more dimensions has some intuitive appeal, because the one dimensional model suggested that there was no advantage in institutions which distinguished themselves, and which stood out from the crowd. At least within the multidimensional model, extreme and innovative positions are not at any particular disadvantage, but it seems that nothing can be said about the area in which preferred choices are likely to fall. In the political studies that have been concluded, party platforms show a stability and well-defined difference which is inconsistent with the theory – stability being in conflict with 'chaos theory', and well-defined difference being in conflict with 'median voter theorem'. It can reasonably be assumed that in competitive situations there will be a predictable spread of profiles over a fairly well defined range. It is therefore necessary to look at a number of the theoretical developments designed to ensure that theory provides a more believable description of events.

To this point, institutions have been treated as anonymous, and interchangeable. It has been assumed that a market position would be adopted solely to secure students and that any market position was equally open to any institution. That is to say that if institution A adopts market position a and institutions B adopts position b, and students are attracted to A, then the position can be reversed by institution B if it adopts position a, leaving institution A to adopt position b.

In almost all practical situations these assumptions will be invalidated by the institutions' commitment to develop a profile *in order to do something specific*, and by a history and reputation which makes it credible in some positions but not in others. For example, suppose that two institutions O and P are seeking extra students in a specific area, and, using the median voter theorem, both decide to base their marketing on the 'access' criterion. If institution O has a history and reputation for access, while institution P has a history and reputation for recruiting 'conventional' students, then the two campaigns will not be equally believable. Indeed, the comparison is far more damaging to institution **P** than the simple credibility of the proposal: it suggests that **P**'s strategy is motivated entirely by fiscal considerations and not at all by policy, philosophical or educational considerations.

Ingberman (1989) has suggested that this issue of history/reputation/credibility occupies a considerable amount of politicians' time, and its importance in the educational processes is signalled by criteria which appear to test exactly this question. For example, institutions try to locate their actions within a broader institutional vision.

The complementary activity, of undermining the opponent's position, also occupies a considerable amount of the attention of politicians. This aspect of the theory suggests that, especially in specialised areas, this may also become a growing concern of academics in the UK, as it has been more publicly in the USA for some time.

These considerations of history and reputation lend a conservative tone to the analysis, and introduce the expectation of more stable patterns of behaviour. Some authors have postulated a mechanism which also restores the central tendency in the special interest group, or political party. In the political analysis, individual candidates select policy positions near formulated bodies of opinion, in order to secure resources to reach a wider public. An analogy would be that institutional policies which fall close to the position of a professional body, political party or commercial interest, might secure additional resources to help in their formulation, or to lobby for their success.

An alternative approach to this problem, adopted by Cox (1989), has been to look for a central subset of the policy area, in which selected institutional profiles are almost certain to lie. The size and nature of this subset, and indeed its very existence, are closely linked to both the overall patterns of preferences of the decision making body, and the process for arriving at aggregate decisions. Further elaboration of distinctions in patterns of preference and decision procedures are therefore unavoidable.

Muddling Towards a Policy

At the heart of the decision theory analysis of such processes of committee decision making is the notion of equilibria. Equilibrium exists when each party to the decision has selected a strategy on the basis of the best information available, and subsequently has no incentive to change that strategy. The strategies which make up the equilibrium position, or solution, may be either pure strategies or mixed strategies. Decision theoreticians are rarely concerned with identifying a specific solution or equilibrium, and are generally concerned with the questions of whether equilibria exist, and if they do exist, in which part of the policy space they exist.

The chaos theorems cited above are typical of this, in the sense that they assert that there is no guarantee that equilibrium solutions do exist. This is because, if we knew which marketing position was winning at the moment, and we had perfect information about the preferences of the committee, we could always submit a proposal which would beat the current winner. Consequently, well-informed institutions would always have an incentive to change their position, and the system could never settle into equilibrium.

But equally intuitively, although there is no guarantee that there will be solutions, it seems probable that somewhere near the centre of a committee's preferences there is an area where equilibrium is likely to exist. This region of policy space is called the 'core', and it is a question of empirical import whether, under any specified pattern of individual preferences of the committee, and any particular voting rule, the core exists, and if it exists, how large it is.

In the empirical study of equilibria, there are two main paths which can be followed. The first is to look at voting rules, and how these affect the size of the core and consequently the strategies of those tendering for funds. The second is to look at patterns of preference and to link the size of the core to properties which are less dependent on specific voting procedures. A combination of these two approaches would, of course, be desirable, but there are considerable difficulties. In the case of a body coming to its conclusion confidentially, information about specific voting rules may not be available, nor may it be possible to analyse the preference of individual members.

Finally, the confidential nature of the proceedings may make any such programme of research impracticable, and it may be necessary to work back from the solution, to speculate about the nature of the processes involved and the properties of the distributions of preferences which generate them. The literature on the application of decision theory to the political field suggests that although these approaches may be interesting, they may not be conclusive.

In looking at specific voting procedures, Cox (1989) has demonstrated that different procedures lead to differences in the size of the core. One consequence of this is that lobby groups can be expected to adopt slightly different strategies under different formulations of majority rule. Broadly speaking, the more restrictive the conditions placed on the voting procedure, the smaller the core, and consequently the more precise the lobbyist needs to be in framing a proposal.

It is not only formal changes in the voting procedure, however, which can lead to differences in competitor strategy. In US presidential elections, it would appear to be obvious that every candidate for office would attempt to maximise his probability of winning, but Grelow and Hinich (1989) have shown that maximising the probability of winning is not the same as maximising one's majority, and a candidate may follow different strategies to reach these two goals. In practice, some of the observed behaviour of candidates makes better sense if viewed in the light of the latter goal rather than the former. In this sense, institutions may have an informal goal which is identifiable separately from the formal procedures, and it would make sense to ask whether such informal targets could be identified.

The core of a round of tendering, if it exists, lies somewhere near the centre of the distribution of individual choices of committee members. But the properties, and especially the size, of the core are sensitive to the voting procedures which are employed. If there is something which can be loosely referred to as 'the general will' of the committee, it will, according to an intuitive notion, lie somewhere near the core. Moreover, it would seem to make sense to talk about a general will without referring to specific voting procedures. A number of authors have therefore focused on areas at the heart of the preference distribution which are independent of the voting procedure. The most obvious example is the Pareto optimal set, which will be familiar to classical economists. Decisions are Pareto optimal if there is no alternative that improves the situation for one group member without making matters worse for another group member. Other sets at the centre of the preference distribution are defined in terms which are more closely related to game theory. The 'uncovered set', or set of all strategies which are not dominated, in the game theoretic sense, would be one such example.

There remains the question whether, on any specific distribution of preferences, the Pareto set or the uncovered set are empty. If they are not empty, a strategy which is in one of those sets must be preferable to one which is not. Since the core is defined as those solutions from which competitors would have no incentive to change, the core must lie inside both of these sets.

Feld, Grofman and Miller (1989) focus attention on a different region of the policy space, called the 'yolk'. Unlike the other regions, the yolk must always exist. McKelvey has linked the size of the yolk to various other properties of the preference distribution, and in particular to the uncovered set.

Feld *et al.* argue that the yolk plays a significant part in limiting the control of one with the power to set the agenda. The chaos theorems of Downs and others suggest that an agenda setter with perfect knowledge of the preferences of individuals, and with control over the order in which the agenda is taken, can effectively produce any outcome they please. While the formal proof of that theorem cannot be avoided, Feld *et al.* argue that movement towards the yolk is easier to achieve than movement away from the yolk. One can, by imposing some fairly modest restrictions on the agenda setter, ensure that the outcome lies very close to the yolk. In the political context, the restriction that the present policy or *status quo* must enter into the selection at the final stage is one such, although it is not immediately obvious what the corresponding stipulation in a tendering system would be, where all tenders represent 'new' contracts. However, it also follows that any imperfection in the knowledge or control of the agenda setter would be most strongly felt in attempts to move away from the yolk. Feld *et al.* therefore suggest that in real life solutions the size and location of the yolk are likely to be crucial in determining which solutions are possible.

Empirical studies of US presidential elections have confirmed this tendency for solutions to lie near the centre of the policy space defined by individual voter preferences. Analysts differ, however, as to whether solutions simply lie in the centre, or around the centre, with a positively excluded hole in the centre. Considerable empirical study of the bidding process would be needed to determine the precise implications for the institutions involved.

The conclusion which one arrives at by looking at these considerations of group behaviour is that group decisions are quite different from the decisions of the individuals who make them up. In particular the final choice of a committee or other corporate body may not be determined and a judicious agenda-setter may be able to move the committee through a sequence of steps towards any particular goal that they choose. The result is that a combination of simple individual preferences when added together produces complex behaviour. The three with whom I started this discussion of Condorcet's paradox and Arrow's theorem moved from the choice of one bottle of wine to another, to another and then back to where they started and they are doomed to circle indecisively forever unless one of them changes their mind. Larger committees with more complex patterns of preferences may not pass exactly the same way a second time but may circle through decisions, generally speaking moving towards the yolk with greater ease than they move away from it.

I have referred to this conclusion as a chaotic consequence and I will take this up more fully in Chapter 10 when I look at complex systems. However, at this point I simply remark that the path of this committee through the decision space can be seen to resemble the strange attractor of chaos theory. It can also be seen that the omniscient agenda-setter is taking advantage of the butterfly effect although, as I will examine in more detail in Chapter 10, ultimately the butterfly effect undermines this notion of omniscience.

Not all educationally interesting groups are formally constituted as committees. Other groups work by informal methods of decision making or no explicit decision making at all, as with classes and seminar groups. However, many of the considerations which arise in the context of formal committees also arise in less formal settings although the exact workings of those decision making processes and methods of arriving at group preferences will be more difficult to determine and harder to predict.

Any experienced teacher will know that classes and seminar groups are easier to steer in some directions than in others and their behaviour may appear to be strongly influenced by considerations which the teacher might regard as irrelevant. In the context of classroom discipline I am reminded of a group which I taught very early on in my teaching career, last thing on a Wednesday afternoon and first thing on a Thursday morning.

The pupils arrived for their class exhausted after an energetic physical education class on Wednesday afternoon and were fractious and relatively uninterested in studying their science. On Thursday morning they were an entirely different class even though my preparation of material and structuring of class discipline may have been very similar. I would like to think that the key determinants of classroom discipline were the content of the class and my ability to set out a lesson and that the state of exhaustion of the pupils was in that sense irrelevant. On the other hand, I came to recognise that it was probably the most relevant element in the classroom setting when it came to deciding group preferences for activities.

CHAPTER TEN: CHAOS AND COMPLEXITY

The crux to formulating well-founded theories in the field of Education Studies is to find a way of representing a partial articulation, or a limited autonomy, between the different levels of understanding. That is to say, we have to find a way of leaving room for individual choice and free will, while admitting that those same choices are shaped by and adapted to the social settings in which individuals find themselves .

I have presented two solutions in some detail. In game theory analysis, group behaviours are described, without limiting the scope for an individual's decision. In linear programming, policy frameworks are described without the imposition of deterministic models. In both cases links to chaos theory have been suggested, but it is in chaos theory itself that this partial autonomy finds its clearest expression.

This naturally leads one to examine institutions, not in terms of the mechanistic, clockwork models of classical mechanics, but in terms of new models of complexity taken from the physical sciences. Chaos theory, or complexity theory, is becoming something of a vogue in management sciences and social science. However, the insights which are drawn from complexity are often interpreted through the lens of classical mechanics, and therefore rendered incorrect in the application. Chaos and complexity theory is examined in greater detail in this chapter.

Systems thinking has taken a dominant position in the development of educational systems, and in the shaping of educational theory. It has become commonplace to look upon teachers as 'inputs' to the educational process, and examination results as 'outputs'. It has also, unfortunately, become commonplace to think that educational institutions can be improved by introducing quality assurance mechanisms which would be more appropriate in a sausage factory. Anybody who doubts the pervasiveness of systems theory might look at a website which specialises in links to systems theory sites; www.uni-klu.ac.at/users/gossimit/links/bookmksd.htm is by no means alone.

The idea of a "system" where one feeds raw material in at one end and collects finished products at the other is deeply rooted in a nineteenth century imagination, dominated by the steam engine, or the factory production line. It is part of the same imagination which motivated an attempt to define learning in terms of stimulus and response; if we can manage the stimuli and the inputs properly, we can secure regular and predictable outcomes. In systems thinking the emphasis is upon teaching, classroom management, and performance indicators.

Such attempts to transfer understanding from the physical sciences to the social sciences have not been successful. Everyone who has ever taught knows that education cannot be controlled and regulated in this way. If a hundred people attend a lecture, they will all learn something different, depending upon the experiences which they bring with them. What is learnt is only loosely connected to what is taught, even more remotely connected to the title of the lecture or the subject attached to a timetabled class, and most remotely connected to the mission statement of the institution. A theoretical imagination of the educational process needs to recognise this partial autonomy between levels within an institution.

In this chapter I will set out an alternative vision of how to understand the educational process, drawn from chaos theory. This model recognises that what happens at different levels are connected but not mutually determined. It also recognises that organisations are not merely the sum of the individuals who make them up. Although not strictly empirical, this chapter points towards some of the practical implications, and the ways in which this different model would shape research and management approaches in education.

A valuable first step has already been taken in this direction by Tsoukas (1998: 297) who contrasts the old, Newtonian style, which has informed a mechanical, controlling approach to the study of organisations, with a Chaotic style. The Newtonian style, which includes systems approaches, places emphasis upon hierarchy within systems, upon control, and upon detailed specification of the parts of systems.

Tsoukas (1998:297) goes on to argue that "The world envisioned by chaos theory differs significantly from the Newtonian view", primarily because it conceives of organisations as developed through mutual influence and interaction, rather than through command and control. System-thinking is part of the modern or positive approach of transferring deterministic scientific approaches to the understanding of educational situations. In contrast, a chaos theory approach emphasises that there are iterative feedback loops, with teachers influencing students, students influencing students and students influencing teachers, but none of them absolutely determining the responses of the others. Influence without determinism suggests that there is partial autonomy between the different levels within an organisation.

The process of modelling using chaos theory must go beyond the simple assertion that organisations are complex, or that they demonstrate some of the features of chaos theory. Chaos theory includes an understanding of how those features are to be interpreted, and work is necessary to elaborate the models more carefully and to demonstrate that the insights of chaos theory are valuable. In Tsoukas (1998: 305) words "Analogies are not discovered; they are constructed".

To develop an account of chaotic behaviour, I draw upon ideas I first put forward some time ago (Turner 1992) and which are developed more fully in Hall (1991) and Gleick (1998).

Tsoukas (1998: 305) identifies the key concepts which chaos theory has to offer:

> "Chaos and complexity theory draw our attention to certain features of organisations about which organisation theorists were, on the whole, only subliminally aware. Notions like *nonlinearity, sensitivity to initial conditions, iteration, feedback loops, novelty, unpredictability, process* and *emergence* make up a new vocabulary in terms of which we may attempt to redescribe organisations".

The issues of emergence and iteration, sensitivity to initial conditions, feedback loops, and unpredictability, are developed in the following section, in a way which will facilitate the application of those concepts to the study of educational institutions.

Emergence and Iteration

Figure 10.1: Part of the Mandelbrot Set

The root of the ideas of emergence and iteration lie in fractal geometry, graphically illustrated in Figure10.1. Each part of the pattern could be magnified (see Figure 10.3), and would show continuing complexity. Magnifying the pattern a thousand or even a million times would not bring us to simple patterns.

Fractals take many forms, from strictly geometrical patterns, to tree-shaped patterns, and to these very beautiful patterns illustrated by the Mandelbrot set. But they all have this in common, that within a finite space (such as the rectangle containing Figure 10.1) there are infinite varieties of patterns, and an infinite regress into detail. One can grasp the overall pattern at a glance, but the whole can never be grasped because attention to detail in one area reveals further subdivision of the pattern. Understanding the full richness of the pattern requires dipping into the details at different 'magnifications' and returning to the overall picture, with an understanding of each 'level' illuminating the picture at other levels.

In institutional terms, the various levels of complex understanding can only be achieved by 'dipping into' study at different levels and carrying insights between levels. Institutions have goals and missions, explicit or implicit, and these impact upon the departmental policy, and personal targets and ambitions, in different ways. But equally, personal actions and departmental objectives impact upon institutional goals and possibilities. Achieving a 'full' understanding of institutional patterns will require a cycle of examinations moving between the institutional organisation chart, through departmental interactions to the individual, and perhaps beyond to the complex and sometimes contradictory motivation of individuals, and back again. Better understandings can be achieved through successive cycles or iterations, as policy and action themselves will be influenced by diverse influences within the system.

This does not completely invalidate the large view, taken at low magnification. The overall pattern can be grasped at a glance, and cannot be completely understood by any amount of detailed scrutiny of the detail. Fractal patterns, like organisations, exhibit emergent properties which are not simply the sum of their parts. A complex organisation is more than the sum of its parts.

When an individual performs an institutional function, such as chairing a meeting or teaching a class, they simultaneously fulfil an institutional role, respond to reactions and expectations of other participants in structured ways, and balance their own motivations and drives. These various activities cannot be understood separately, any more than they can be reduced one to another.

Understanding an institution as a complex organisation therefore draws attention to the need to understand specific actions and processes in context - and one might include an internal context in addition to an external one. Complex organisations can be contrasted with simple command and control systems where messages/instructions are disseminated from the top. In complex organisations messages may be transmitted but how they are received or implemented will depend upon local contexts.

Feedback Loops

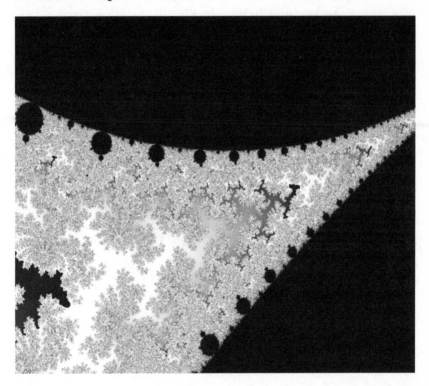

Figure 10.2: A small part of Figure 10.1 magnified many hundreds of times

Figure 10.2 illustrates a very tiny part of Figure 10.1 magnified to show great detail. Such patterns cannot be generated by design or by the detailed specification of each element of the pattern, but are the result of relatively simple calculations which are repeated with feedback from one level to another. This closely parallels processes which we recognise as taking place in large educational organisations. A relatively simple goal, such as the introduction of performance targets, can be set in motion, but each of the parts of the organisation and the individuals in it will interact to produce differentiated effects by operating upon each other throughout the implementation process.

That underlying simplicity is reflected, however, in the fact that patterns at different levels in fractal patterns show certain similarities, or recursive symmetries. Fractal patterns are self-similar, while showing great differences between them, as a comparison of Figures 10.1 and 10.3 illustrates. We might therefore expect the mathematics departments to show stronger similarities to the English department and science department in their own school than they do to mathematics departments in general. The self-similarities of fractal patterns suggest a way of approaching such complex issues as 'school ethos' consisting of subtly different interpretations of common approaches. This is a conclusion which is open to empirical examination, and which bears directly upon efforts to develop 'whole school' policies.

Figure 10.3: A Fractal as a Representation of Nature

Attention has been drawn to the similarities between some fractals and naturally occurring patterns of recursive symmetry, such as the structure of a fern, or the piles of rocks on mountainsides. We are relatively comfortable with the idea that some systems have features which recur at different levels of aggregation. We know that many patterns of behaviour have a tendency to be cyclical – abused children raising abused families, bullied people turning into bullies. Within an organisation there will be a tendency for communication styles adopted at one level to be replicated at other levels, so that whole organisations can be either abusive or caring, without any necessary causal link between the principal's behaviour and the behaviour of teachers in the classroom.

This notion of recursive symmetry might therefore offer an interesting tool in examining school culture.

This property that the whole can be reflected in each of the parts is a direct and obvious corollary of the involvement of fractal geometry. It has been described by Morgan (1997) as being a 'holographic' property, in the sense that the entire picture of a holograph is contained in each part of the photographic plate.

Unpredictability

Unpredictability, the difficulty of predicting exactly what a system will do, is linked to the concept of a strange attractor. We are aware of the presence of simple attractors in our everyday experience. A pendulum is pulled back towards the central point of its swing, and that point is a simple attractor. That simple fact, that a pendulum is pulled back towards its central point with a force which is proportional to its distance from the attractor, is enough to define the movement of the pendulum. Simple attractors produce simple, cyclical motion which is completely predictable, a fact used in the development of pendulum clocks. Strange attractors are similar, but not quite the same.

It is relatively easy to make a practical system that demonstrates a strange attractor. For purposes of demonstration, I use a length of string with two masses attached to it; one at the bottom end and one about halfway down. When this system is set in motion, its behaviour is more or less periodic, but only more or less.

The path of the lower mass is a strange attractor. The most famous strange attractor in the literature is the Lorenz attractor, which is shown in Figure 10.4. Again, in Figure 10.4 one can see the imperfect periodic motion depicted as a path which never quite returns to its starting point.

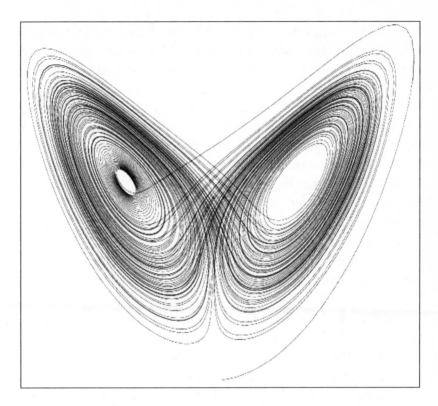

Figure 10.4: The Lorenz Attractor

The notion of the pendulum as metaphor in understanding organisations has had a common, one might almost say hypnotic, effect on thinking "The pendulum has swung towards X over the last five years, and can be expected to swing back soon".

Sensitivity to Initial Conditions, or The Butterfly Effect

The butterfly effect is one of the most famous outcomes of chaos theory, but equally perhaps one of the most misunderstood. Because there is a lack of predictability in strange attractors, relatively small errors in specifying the starting conditions of the system can lead to very large errors in predictions about where it will be in the future. Or, to put it in the example which gave the effect its name, the flap of a

171

butterfly's wing in the Amazon\China\Madagascar can lead to a hurricane in Texas\Australia\Japan. The reader is free to substitute any other locations which seem preferable.

There is an inherent attraction in the notion of the butterfly effect, as it touches upon our experience of human motivation. We can perhaps think of instances where a startling idea or a few words or a brief experience have been enough to start what turns out to be a lifetime's work. Einstein claimed that his interest in forces started from the childhood gift of a magnet, which had fascinated him. Even if that story is apocryphal, it appears plausible, and captures something about the way in which passions can begin from chance events.

The weather system of the globe is extremely complex, with many feedback loops, and is inherently chaotic. The literal butterfly effect has implications for predicting and modelling the patterns of weather. If something as small as the flap of an insect's wing can have massive effects, what should weather forecasters do? At first sight, and in classical mode, it looks as though this places a demand for greater accuracy in specifying the starting position of the weather pattern; if we are to make valid predictions of the weather, we will need to know the location of every butterfly. But it is important to recognise that this is not just a practically insurmountable problem. It is not a theoretically plausible response either. Butterflies are not the only thing which might create a slight weather disturbance; butterfly nets and infra-red butterfly detectors may also produce minor perturbations in air flow. Attempts to determine precisely the initial condition of a complex system will themselves disturb those initial conditions, and invalidate predictions. The goal of a perfectly specified starting position from which to make predictions is not just difficult, it is impossible. In just the same way, it would be impossible to describe Figure 10.1 by specifying the infinitely subdivided detail which makes it up. The butterfly effect and the nature of fractals are intimately interconnected.

Maguire and McKelvey (1999: 9) note that metaphors in the literature of organisations and complexity theory are widespread, and that,

> "while metaphors are applauded, a number of reviewers feel that authors' over-reliance on metaphors contributes to 'superficial' treatments".

In this context, it may be helpful to distinguish between different kinds of uses of metaphors ranging along a spectrum.

At the most superficial end, one would find metaphors which were based upon nothing more than linguistic similarity. Chaos theory, or as some writers prefer complexity theory, deals with a number of fairly tightly defined, linked concepts, as set out above. Simply because we apply the term 'complex' to an organisation or phenomenon, it does not necessarily follow that that organisation or phenomenon displays the features described by complexity theory. In particular, if one of the features of complexity theory is lifted out of context, and applied in an understanding which is primarily in 'Newtonian style', the result can simply be wrong. This will be illustrated below in more detail.

At the other end of the spectrum one would find formal modelling techniques, where a specific, idealised organisation would be described in terms of hypothetical properties, and the model developed to show the features which could not necessarily be intuited. That idealised model could then be compared with actual institutions to test whether the insights afforded by the model improved understanding of observed phenomena. This remains 'metaphorical' in the sense that a direct apprehension of whether an organisation *is* chaotic is impossible. But it resembles the methods of the physical sciences, where the same mathematical models are used to describe gravitational, magnetic and electrical fields.

Between these two extremes is an intermediate area, where models are partially developed, or developed in qualitative terms, and where valuable insights can be gathered. Such applications might also indicate ways in which more rigorous modelling might be useful.

Complexity and Management

Maguire and McKelvey (1999) suggest that the application of chaos theory to organisations is likely to become a fad, unless it can be moved along that spectrum towards the more developed modelling mode.

Griffin, Shaw and Stacey (1998: 325) cite the critique offered by Shotter (1993) of Morgan's use of chaos theory. Morgan (1997: 271) takes the concept of the butterfly effect, that small influences can have huge effects, and, fitting it into a managerial approach which is conceived primarily in the Newtonian style, concludes that this offers a useful management tool:

> "...it follows that any person wishing to change the context in which they are operating should search for 'doable' high leverage initiatives that can trigger a transition from one attractor to another".

Griffin, Shaw and Stacey (1998: 325) argue that,

> "We can hear how Morgan speaks with the objectifying, controlling and individual agency voice about complexity",

a voice which they argue is inappropriate for the insights which chaos theory offers concerning collective interaction in producing outcomes.

There is, however, a stronger criticism of Morgan which is available, which is that anybody who believes that the butterfly effect can be used in the purposeful way proposed by Morgan has simply failed to understand the butterfly effect.

To see that this is true, one might imagine a teacher in a classroom seeking information about the precise timing of an intervention in order to have a 'high-leverage' effect. Such a teacher will be assessing students' readiness to learn, evaluating relationships between pupils, and so on. The attempt to specify the initial conditions with the degree of accuracy necessary is bound to interfere with the teaching process itself. And the impact of such overt testing may have an impact upon the general social climate of the classroom, changing the conditions, and making quite other interventions appropriate. The butterfly effect cannot be exploited in planning interventions into the educational process.

Moving away from such superficial approaches to the application of chaos theory, Eve, Horsfall and Lee (1997) include a number of examples which represent social situations diagrammatically, and the similarity between some of the diagrams and the Lorenz attractor are compelling. For example, Alisch, Azizighanbari and Bargfeldt (1997) model the dynamics of children's friendships, and one can see in their diagrams aspects which would appear to be similar to strange attractors. However, as Alisch *et al.* argue, there is no way of working out from a finite amount of data whether what we are observing is indeed a strange attractor.

What is evident from these applications is that there are systems which appear to exhibit some of the characteristics of chaos, and that valuable insights can be achieved. In particular, it makes sense, as Alisch, Azizighanbari and Bargfeldt (1997) argue, to try to control conditions which dispose systems towards chaotic or non-chaotic behaviour, such as the number of interrelated variables or feedback loops within a system, but it makes no sense to try to predict the path of chaotic development once chaos is established.

The intuition or insight which is offered by a complexity science approach to organisation theory differs sharply here from that offered by traditional managerial approaches in the Newtonian style. In the letter, it is supposed that the operation of an organisation is the sum of its parts, in which case it is necessary to establish complete control over the action of each individual in order to achieve organisational goals. What follows is the development of ever tighter, possibly coercive, mechanisms to ensure compliance with institutional policies. The insight offered by chaos theory is that such a process is unlikely to be successful in eliminating chaotic responses, and that other approaches, such as the reduction of feedback loops between levels, or a more diffuse approach to organisational culture, are likely to be equally effective, if not more effective. One can understand moves towards flatter organisational structures (reducing the number of feedback loops) or total quality management (addressing the overall pattern without trying to control every detail) in these terms. While these examples are retrospective, and do not add very much new in themselves, one can begin to see how chaos theory might offer new ways of looking at managerial issues.

Moving further along the spectrum towards formal modelling, Passerini and Bahr (1997) offer a different approach. Essentially, they define an artificial system (an automaton model) which has individual features which are assumed to be analogous to human decision making. The whole system can be seen to be chaotic, and one can therefore apply the metaphor more directly to actual social systems. Such an approach offers more hope that the analysis will lead to valuable insights, whereas the earlier approach of Alisch *et al.* can never really hope to go beyond the casually interesting.

To go beyond this, it will be necessary to develop more fully articulated models of strange attractors in educational settings, rather than simply relying upon the force of metaphors. This is a question I shall return to when applications of chaos theory are considered.

Fortunately, there are models which have been developed in other contexts which can help in this process of developing models of complex organisation. In particular, a good deal of work has been done on decision making processes which involve large numbers of people. These have already been examined at some length in Chapter 9. In exploring the models for the behaviour of committees, Turner and Pratt (1990) drew upon a body of decision theory which is rooted in game theory. One of the important results from that field is the fact that the preferences of any group of more than three people may not be transitive. One would think an individual odd if they said to us "I prefer red wine over white wine, and I prefer rosé wine over red wine, but I prefer white wine over rosé". The expectation is that if red wine is preferable to white wine, and rosé wine is preferable to red wine, then rosé wine must be preferable to white wine. When one considers the preferences of an individual, one expects this logical ordering, or in other words one expects that preferences are transitive, and that there is a pecking order, where establishing that rosé wine is higher than red wine in the pecking order also establishes that it is higher than everything below red in the pecking order.

However, when we consider the preferences of groups, things can be very different. Groups of three or more people are quite likely to have preferences which are not transitive, and the likelihood of such an outcome increases dramatically the more people are involved in contributing to the choice. One of the most important results of game theory considerations of aggregating the preferences of individuals is Arrow's theorem, which states that there is no system of decision making which can ensure that the group's preferences are transitive, at the same time as meeting certain other minimal criteria.

For example, one of Arrow's conditions is that the decision making process must not be a dictatorship. If the group's decisions are always the same as the decisions of the chair person (or any other individual) then one would expect those decisions to demonstrate the transitivity of preferences.

Within the realm of decision theory, game theory and voting theory, this leads to a further conclusion. Since within a large group preferences may not be transitive, it will be possible to arrive at paradoxical situations where the group will 'go round in circles' preferring first one option, then a second, then a third, and coming back to the first option, or something very near to it. Imagine a large committee, such as a board of directors or university's academic board, trying to decide a plan, for example to invest amount X in one area and an amount Y in another. Assuming that the preferences of the committee are non-transitive, then whatever the present plan on the table, an omniscient agenda-setter could find a configuration which would be preferable, and then another and another. Over time, such an agenda-setter could manoeuvre the committee along a decision trail. If we plotted a graph of X and Y over time, the result might look very like Figure 10.4.

This in itself is a very interesting result, as it tells us that democratic, collective and collegial institutions are inherently liable to chaos, and that as a result they are in equal measure protected from manipulation.

A common conclusion from the above result is that such democratic processes are essentially flawed, in that an omniscient agenda-setter could lead the committee by the nose to whatever conclusion was desired. There are two contrary conclusions, however, which follow from chaos theory. If it is going to be possible for the all-knowing manipulator to lead the committee absolutely anywhere (as opposed to simply going around in circles) then the process must be chaotic, and the path through the policy space must be a strange attractor. And if that is the case, as pointed out in Turner (1992), consideration of the butterfly effect tells us that 'omniscience' is not even theoretically available. The omniscient agenda-setter is a convenient fiction, and any confusion of that fiction with an actual person leads to the invalid conclusion which Morgan (1997) arrived at that a controlling manager can use the butterfly effect to their advantage.

But the result developed here goes far beyond that, because it suggests that decision models drawn from game theory can lead to patterns best described by chaos theory, and thereby establish a strong link between game theory and chaos theory in describing group behaviour.

Game theory and chaos theory have something else in common which is perhaps more important. In looking at certain games, there are circumstances in which long runs of 'plays' exhibit strong patterns, while individual 'plays' are, and must be, completely unpredictable. (Or, which is theoretically equivalent, if many individuals make one 'play' each, groups will be predictable but individuals will not.) The fast bowler in cricket may bowl one bouncer in every six deliveries, but if the batsman can tell when it is coming, the effect is wasted. The pitcher in baseball may throw a curve ball twenty per cent of the time with great regularity, but it should never be possible to tell what the next ball will be. And the tennis player who always plays to the opponent's backhand, however weak that backhand is, is losing the weapon of surprise. Thus game theory looks for predictability in group behaviour, but has nothing to say on individual behaviour.

Classroom situations are not formal committees. But neither are they dictatorships. A teacher may be able to command certain norms of behaviour, but is not able to dictate what will be learned. Tolstoy argued that if every soldier in Napoleon's army had dropped his rifle and refused to march, Napoleon would not have been able to advance on Moscow. In much the same way, teachers depend upon the tacit compliance of their pupils. Although there may not be formal resolutions and voting procedures, classroom atmosphere is the result of group decision making rather than dictat. True, mechanical, dictatorship is much rarer than systems theory would have us believe.

Complexity and a Reassertion of Values

Consideration of the question of partial autonomy between levels in an educational system suggests that the introduction of chaos theory permits two apparently contradictory insights into the way organisations can be understood. Mention has already been made of the emphasis which is placed upon linking between levels of understanding. On the other hand, the consideration of fractal geometry also leads to an understanding of emergence, that there are patterns at one level which are not determined by, and cannot be reduced to, patterns at another. This leaves a space within the theory for human individuality and idiosyncrasy. Not surprisingly, this leads to new insights into the place of the individual within the organisation.

Tsoukas (1998: 300-301) remarks that,

"It is worth noticing how the impossibility of prediction invites us to reconsider the concept of *freedom*, which has long been ignored in a mechanistically inclined social science. In a deterministic world, a world of known causes leading to predictable effects, freedom makes no sense. A mechanistic social science modelled on Newtonian physics does not need freedom".

In other words, the new style of thinking makes it possible to reintroduce human aspects which have had no place in mechanical or biological models.

Maguire and McKelvey (1999: 40) state that,

"there seems to be a significant coalition forming... within the 'complexity and management' community emphasizing and promoting 'humanistic' organisational development. Several authors invoke complexity science to authorize and legitimate increased worker freedom, tolerance, the acceptance of dissent, increased communication, sharing of information, and such things as the building of emotional involvement, personal commitment, community, etc. In addition, the phenomena of trust and social capital reappear in books and reviews. Whether complexity science, in fact, supports these claims is moot at this juncture".

The resurgence of interest in the humanistic can be seen as an integral aspect of chaos theory, and not an accidental adjunct. The attention which chaos theory draws to interlinking between levels simultaneously emphasises a de-coupling of levels; no one level determines any other. Linear causation has been removed, in order to leave clearly defined areas of indeterminacy which allow us to think of individual agency and humanistic values within institutional contexts.

This can be seen graphically in Figure 10.1. One is struck by certain overwhelming symmetries and patterns. Somewhere, occupying less than a square millimetre, slightly above the centre line and towards the left of the figure, is the pattern which, when magnified makes up Figure 10.2. But the presence of that complexity at the micro-level does not detract from the patterns we observe at the macro-level.

We can therefore envisage developing models for organisations where macro-level regularities are not based upon corresponding determined relationships at the micro-level. At a very important level this corresponds to an obvious feature of social organisations; predictions of groups are very much easier than predictions of individuals. It is easier to predict the outcome of an election than the voting behaviour of individual electors. Indeed, predicting the outcome of an election would be impossible if it involved the summation of the prediction of individual votes cast. It is easier to predict traffic jams than to predict which cars will be stuck in them. It is easier to predict long term trends in markets than to predict which individuals will be buying which products at which time. We can have a clear grasp of trends at a macro-level of society, without feeling the need to understand everything at the micro-level.

This property from game theory and chaos theory, of loose articulation between the micro- and macro-levels, suggest that they have much to offer on the analysis of social organisations, especially educational institutions. Although, in practice, modelling in the Newtonian style has been forced to accept, for pragmatic reasons, a failure to account for individual difference and choice in stochastic models, such indeterminacy is usually accounted for in terms of 'error' or current shortcomings in actual models. In the models of complexity, lack of determinacy is embraced as an integral and positive feature of the models, which opens up possibilities in the understanding of human interaction.

The real prospect is even brighter than that offered by the models to be found in the literature at present, because the argument developed here suggests that it will be possible to develop models of institutions which leave great indeterminacy at the individual level. Learning cannot be promoted by treating it as mechanically determined. Chaos theory provides a way of understanding processes where individual responses are shaped, but not determined, by group activity. But the notion of recursive symmetry suggests that chaotic pockets are unlikely to occur in rigidly controlled institutions. Applying the Newtonian imagination to educational institutions, and insisting upon complete predictability and accountability, is likely to squeeze out areas of creative chaos. In practical terms this has been understood by educationists such as Homer Lane and A.S.Neill, who insisted that education could only be promoted within democratic organisations, and as noted above, democratic organisations have an inherent tendency towards chaotic features.

More needs to be done in developing this alternative way of conceptualising educational institutions. We know how to prevent chaotic behaviour in systems. The complex pendulum described above can be made perfectly determined, and will fit into the Newtonian framework, if only its two parts are separated and analysed independently. In much the same way, the chaos inherent in a democratic organisation can be removed by imposing a dictatorship, a single command and control structure. Managing 'enough' chaos within flexible frameworks is a much more demanding challenge, and one which is desperately needed for education in the 21st century.

Archer (1995) has identified the question of links between the macro- and the micro-levels of sociological analysis as presenting the major challenge to sociological theorists, and also the area where there is most difficulty. However, in presenting her 'morphogenetic' approach, she appears to be locked into the use of causal relationships as the only plausible candidate for understanding those links. Chaos theory offers a different model in which the links between levels are seen as recursive symmetries in complex systems, rather than the result of mechanical links.

This chapter has presented an outline of chaos theory, or complexity theory, as it might be applied to educational institutions. It has been shown how chaos theory brings together from game theory and linear programming certain themes. The most important of these themes are the concepts of emergence and partial autonomy between levels.

I have been at pains to stress the importance of the loose linkage between patterns at different levels, because it conforms to the criterion for good theory that I have suggested, namely that there must be space for individual agency within organisational theory. I am not alone in noting that chaos theory has been linked to concepts of freedom and humanism. The importance of such a framework for understanding human behaviour appears to be compelling.

CHAPTER ELEVEN: CONCLUSIONS

In looking at the parallels between my own experience of science and social science, and the broader developments within the field, it seems to me that there are some important lessons to be learned. In particular, I would say that there were some crucial points where I might have stopped moving forwards. I am less sanguine about the way in which those potential sticking points, points where one could have remained forever in a blind alley, have been dealt with by the theory of Education Studies in a wider sense.

In the first place, and of crucial importance, there was modernism. Modernism is the idea that science can provide all the answers, and that scientific method, properly applied, can move us forward to a complete understanding. It is particularly seductive. But I think that it is also important to engage with the positive side of this experience – like it or loathe it, science has provided some extraordinarily powerful tools for understanding our environment.

The second major step, and temptation to remain fixed, came with an understanding of the flaws of science, and the fact that science cannot do what we hope it will, or what many scientists promise us that it can. However, one of the difficulties with the development of Education Studies is that too many writers have arrived at the critique of modernism, without any real engagement with modernism in the first place. There can all too often be a rejection of science, of scientific method and of anything that has a vaguely scientific pedigree. The result is an iconoclastic approach to theory, with very little positive to offer, and this smacks more of a residue of Snow's two cultures than it does of a positive attempt to move the area forwards.

We have the science and mathematics educated researchers who promote statistical, quantitative methods on the one hand. And on the other hand, we have the arts educated researchers who promote qualitative methods. The two groups do not appear, to date, to have found a language in which to engage in constructive dialogue.

And finally there is a mature concern for the ethical implications of theory, and of the role which power plays in deciding between competing theories. However, once again there is a trap in this position, a trap which I would say was most clearly summarised as a postmodern position. Postmodernism focuses upon the power relationships between theory makers; theories of powerful people are powerful theories. But this understanding alone is enough to remove the theoretical power, or legitimacy, of those theories. The result is again a frozen inactivity, while we wait for open and non-oppressive discourse, and the realisation of better theories. In order to overcome this difficulty, one needs to take a broader view of the ethical issues, not only in relation to competing theories, but also in relation to theorists and those they theorise about. One needs to examine the ethical issues of theorising as such.

At each of these stages there is an important insight to be gained, and a temptation to remain fixed with that partial insight. Scaling each peak, there is a temptation to rest and admire the view, with little incentive and no obvious way to move on further.

The result is one form or another of arrested theoretical development. What I have tried to do here is to take the view from each of those three peaks, and put them together to provide a synoptic view which transcends the difficulties of each. And I have tried to offer examples of what the next steps would be like.

As I have also noted, it is not easy to go very far along that future road, because data is collected to test/illustrate the theories we have. As a result, new theories require new data in order to develop – in Kuhn's terms a period of normal science to follow a scientific revolution. But I recognise the need to do what can be done with current data to give an indication of where those new theories should lead us.

In this final chapter, I shall revisit each of those peaks in turn, and show how the insights they offer can provide a framework which allows us to transcend the present difficulties of theory in Education Studies. Bringing those three theoretical perspectives together is an attempt at grand narrative of exactly the kind that postmodernists would prohibit. Grand narrative may not be very convincing, but attempts at grand narrative are the only hope that we have of moving forward.

One of the features of research in Education Studies that was identified by Tooley (1998) was the prevalence of partisan research, where the researcher used the data to support a specific theoretical position. This is encouraged when the field is divided into different camps, or busy scaling quite separate peaks. If the field is divided in this way, researchers may only talk to researchers of a similar disposition. The obvious antidote is to encourage discussion between researchers who work in very different traditions. Such a transformation of the field of Education Studies cannot be achieved by incremental means; small improvements and movements uphill will only move us towards the local peak. If we seek to move on towards higher peaks still we need to take a synoptic view of the field as a whole. That is what I shall attempt in this chapter.

Modernism

At the root of modernism is the idea that by taking a rational approach and using methods from the physical sciences we can come to a clear understanding of our social world. This ambition has found various forms of expression particularly in the management of organisations.

An early attempt was made by Frederick W Taylor to understand factories in terms of 'scientific management'. (Brown, 1954: 12-14) This led to time and motion studies and a quest for efficiency on the basis of rational planning.

Although that particular attempt was discredited especially by the work of Elton Mayo and his work on the Hawthorn factory of Western Electric, the basic principle persisted that a scientific understanding could be brought about through a rational approach to planning.

What we learned from the studies of Elton Mayo and his colleagues was that people do not respond in simple ways to the stimuli which are provided for them (Brown, 1954: 69-80). In the Hawthorn experiments, for example, lighting was increased for electrical assemblers in an effort to see whether their productivity went up when their work places were better lit. The result was that productivity did rise but when the lighting was reduced again to its earlier levels, far from dropping back, productivity rose yet again. At the heart of social systems are human beings who have intentions, will power and feelings which contribute to the way that those individuals respond to external stimuli.

There are two ways forward from this particular impasse. The one is to say that we need better and better statistical methods in order to be able to predict how humans will behave, and the second is to reject such approaches to understandings of human situations altogether. This simple choice in how to proceed from the difficulties arising over trying to apply scientific methods to understanding people leads to a lasting schism is social science.

Attempts to improve the statistical models have led to large-scale survey and quantitative techniques to describe the behaviour of groups of people. As will be clear from what I have said in earlier chapters, I am of the opinion that this attempt to improve statistical techniques is ultimately doomed because the models used do not leave explicit room for free will in their description of human activities. However before moving on to the critique of modernism which is offered by opponents of large-scale quantitative techniques it is probably as well to remind ourselves of the successes of this area of study.

Modern statistics in terms of social survey techniques originated at the end of the nineteenth century in actuarial work done for insurance companies. In descriptive terms we know much more about the way that people behave than we did at the end of the nineteenth century and this form of descriptive statistics has contributed greatly to that understanding. Most of what we claim to know about educational systems in fact derives from this tradition. A huge amount has been invested in collecting statistics about educational performance and when any report claims that schools make a greater contribution to educational performance than home background, or vice versa, the data is generally derived from such statistical techniques.

It is only when statisticians have gone on to attempt to describe the causes for particular actions that they have come unstuck. In modelling to identify causes generally speaking relatively poor success has been achieved. To explain their failure, statisticians have generally fallen back on the explanation that human behaviour is too complex for modelling in this way and that they have been unable to include sufficient variables. I have argued that this optimistic view of what quantitative methods can achieve is unfounded and that the real problem with large-scale quantitative surveys is that they do not leave a theoretical place for free will.

If we want to move forward then we need to recognise the shortcomings of such statistical techniques. However we also need to realise that much of the data that we have available to us, and most of the 'common sense' explanations which we accept about how educational systems work, are derived from these techniques. If we simply reject statistical methods and quantitative methods we will be 'throwing the baby out with the bath water'.

Critique of Modernism

The alternative response to the shortcomings of statistical modelling in the social sciences has been to reject scientific paradigms embodied in those quantitative techniques and to stress the importance of qualitative insights which can derive from individual case studies and from individuals reflecting upon their own professional practice. As I have already noted I regard this critique of quantitative methods, and of the claims of science to provide a clear road to the truth, as completely well-founded. In claiming to provide access to an improved understanding of how humans operate in organisations, science as understood in quantitative surveys has claimed far too much.

But at the same time it is necessary to remember that individual case studies and individual reflections upon professional practice cannot provide an appropriate way for studying all forms of educational practice. Individual case studies leave entirely open the question of whether their conclusions can be more widely applied. I may, for example by reflection upon my own professional practice, come to the conclusion that particular groups of students and pupils respond well to particular kinds of teaching or particular ways of arranging the learning environment. But I cannot possibly address in this way the question of whether these conclusions are more widely applicable to other students in other settings and other teachers. Questions about the generalizability of conclusions can only be addressed by the sophisticated use of quantitative techniques.

We are thus left with the conclusion that there are two techniques widely adopted in the study of educational organisations which are both deeply flawed. The one is statistical and quantitative and is valuable for descriptions at the macro-scale and the other is individualistic and qualitative and valuable in describing micro-settings of education.

Returning to the argument which Archer has presented, we have one technique which deals with the macro-level and tends to see the responses of the individual in terms of their macro-setting and we have one technique or group of techniques which concentrates upon the micro-level and is unable to address linkages to the macro-level. In a very sharp and distinctive form, we have what Archer has described as the tendency towards upwards conflation on the one hand and the tendency towards downwards conflation upon the other. It will take more than continued work incrementally upon similar lines to bring about a resolution of that dichotomy. It will take a conscious effort to develop theories which show the linkages between the macro and the micro.

In short, we need a healthy scepticism in approaching both quantitative and qualitative studies. We need to recognise that quantitative studies offer us, on the one hand, large-scale descriptors of macro-events but no insights at the individual level, while qualitative studies, on the other hand, offer us shrewd insights into the nuances of individual behaviour but no insights into linkages with broader macro-level issues.

If we are to advance we need to accept that both approaches have their merits, that both approaches have their shortcomings and that a conscious and responsible effort will need to be made to reconcile those into a larger framework. We should not expect such a framework to emerge through a number of incremental steps.

Postmodernism

It is relatively easy if we stress only the shortcomings of the theoretical models that we have available to see the area of theory in Education Studies as dominated by warring camps and to argue that the prevalence of a particular style of theory owes little to the intrinsic qualities of the theories themselves and much to extraneous circumstances which drive theory. Scientific management has found its way into Educational Studies because of the appointment of particular professors in key posts in particular universities and because such approaches have derived support from funding bodies determined to spread the message of scientific management. We might then explore the activities of the Ford Foundation or the Carnegie Foundation in spreading statistical techniques internationally.

Similarly the pedigree of qualitative methods may be traced through key university departments which support it and funding bodies which have promoted it.

It is a relatively short step from that to the conclusion that the success of theories owes nothing at all to their content and everything to the support which they gain from powerful institutions. To borrow a summary from Marx, "The ruling ideas are the ideas of the ruling classes".

In the end, this leads to an infinite regress which is thoroughly demoralising. The position or quality of a scientific theory is judged, not in accordance with what the theory says, but in accordance with sociological understandings about the support it derives from the social groups. However, the theories which we need in order to develop that understanding of power relations which support the particular theories are as questionable as the content of the theories themselves. Everything is built upon sand and there is nowhere we can draw firm conclusions. This is the position to which postmodernism leads us. There are no valuable theories, only those which are offered by powerful groupings.

While there is considerable merit in that argument it is taking the matter too far to say that the content of theories is completely irrelevant. But we are left with much the same problem as before. Newton, the genius, in an act of individual insight produces an understanding of how the planets move. Or, Newton as the mouthpiece of the bourgeoisie, provides an understanding which allows that class to dominate and exploit not only nature but other classes. And still we do not have the wherewithal, the theoretical framework, with which to reconcile our view of Newton as an individual and as a member of a macro-sociological group.

In an attempt to reconcile this particular difficulty postmodern theory, or at least Habermas, has put forward the notion of an ideal speech situation in which people with equal power debate theoretical issues. We might suppose a Newton stripped of his royal patronage and university position debating with a Descartes similarly stripped of social status. Newton's theories may possibly persist on the strength of their own merits but who can possibly know?

This approach implicitly tries to bring into account ethical considerations as regards the ability of theoreticians to make claims about their relative positions. While accepting many of the criticisms offered of older and more optimistic approaches to the development of theory and while applauding the attempt to bring in ethical considerations, I would argue that in the field of social science, postmodernism does not go nearly far enough. An effort is made to account for the moral position of one theorist vis à vis another. I would argue that it is important to take into account the ethical positions of theorists in relation to those people whose behaviour they describe and in doing so I would argue that an important feature of social theory and theory in Education Studies is that it should acknowledge the role of free will, choice and individual intention in shaping educational events. This is not an easy condition to meet and again I would argue that it requires not incremental advance but reasoned and purposeful development of theories to meet the criteria.

Concluding Remarks

What I have tried to demonstrate throughout this book is the notion that there is much to be learned from the physical sciences which can be transferred to the social sciences and to the development of theory in the area of Education Studies. I have given examples which demonstrate that this is not to be done in a simple-minded or facile way but that attention has to be given to the moral implications of developing theory.

In order to achieve the desired results it is necessary to bring to bear upon the task insights which combine an understanding of the role of theory in the physical sciences, an understanding of why those cannot be directly transferred to the social sciences and a perspective of the ethical requirements of theory development. This cannot be achieved incrementally by adding to what we have but must be developed with purposeful reflection upon the nature of theory.

New theories must get away from an over rigid concern with truth. The truth is secondary to the role of theory in developing a framework within which we can understand as wide a range of phenomena as possible.

But most importantly, theory must not embody the notion that there is one best way of developing one's life and therefore one best way of proceeding through educational systems. Theory must escape from the single-centredness which suggests that individuals with comparable backgrounds and comparable inherited traits will pursue the same pathways through educational systems. Our new range of theories must embody the principle that even with those similarities different individuals may appropriately choose different paths for themselves. That is at the heart of developing moral and ethical theories in educational studies.

I have noted at various points in this book that there are cogent critiques of the theory applied in educational research. From their different perspectives Archer, McNiff, Mortimore and Thomas each offer a diagnosis of what is wrong with theory in Education Studies. They all point to the weakness of theory which is based upon a nineteenth century view of science. In their different ways they point to the need for theory to meet the three criteria that I set out in Chapter 1, that good theory should:

- be ethical in allowing scope for individual free will;

- be multi-centred in allowing that there is more than one correct way to develop one's education career;
- should allow for partial autonomy between levels of understanding; between the individual, the school and society more broadly.

These criteria will not be met by accident, by continuing with research until theories which meet the criteria spring out spontaneously. A thorough-going effort to produce theory of the required standard is necessary. In this book, I have tried to give an indication of what a coherent body of theory would look like. Of course, there is much more to be done, and there are many areas that I have barely touched upon. I trust that the foundation I have offered here will be a stimulus to that future work.

References:

Alisch, Azizighanbari and Bargfeldt (1997) "Dynamics of Children's Friendships" in Eve, R.A., Horsfall, S and Lee, M.E. (eds.) (1997) *Chaos, Complexity and Sociology: Myths, Models and Theories* (London: Sage)

Archer, M.S. (1995) *Realist Social Theory: the Morphogenetic Approach* (Cambridge: Cambridge University Press)

Armitage, P. & Smith, C.S. (1972) "The Controllability: an example" Higher Education Review Vol.5,no.1,pp55-66

Bacharach (1976) *Economics and the Theory of Games* (London; MacMillan)

Barrett-Lennard, G. T. (1998) *Carl Roger's Helping System: Journey and Substance* (London: Sage)

Bassey, M. (2001) "A Solution to the Problem of Generalisation in Educational Research: Fuzzy Prediction", in *Oxford Review of Education*, 27 (1) pp.5-22

Boudon, R. (1986) *Theories of Social Change: A Critical Appraisal* (Cambridge: Polity)

Brown, J.A.C. (1954) *The Social Psychology of Industry* (Harmondsworth: Penguin)

Burstein, L. (1992) *The IEA Study of Mathematics III: Contexts and Outcomes of School Mathematics* (Oxford: Pergamon)

Chia, R. (1998) "From Complexity Science to Complex Thinking: Organisation as Simple Location", in *Organisation* Vol.5, No.3, pp.341-369

Colman, A. (1982) *Game Theory and Experimental Games* (London: Pergamon)

Commission on the Social Sciences (2003) *Great Expectations: the Social Sciences in Britain* (London: Commission on the Social Sciences)

Comte, A. (1999) *Auguste Comte and Positivism: The Essential Writings* (Edited by Gertrud Lenzer) (New Brunswick, N.J.: Transaction Publishers)

Coomber, L.C. & Keeves, J.P, (1973) Science Education in Nineteen Countries: An Empirical Study (London: Wiley)

Cox G.W. (1989) "Undominated Candidate Strategies Under Alternative Voting Rules" in Johnson P.E. (1989) *Formal Theories of Politics: Mathematical Modelling in Political Science* (Oxford: Pergamon Press)

Davenport, W. (1960) *"Jamaican Fishing: A Game Theory Analysis"*, in Mintz, S.W. (Ed) (1960) Papers in Caribbean Anthropology Nos.57-64, 3-11 (New Haven, Con.: Yale University Publications in Anthropology)

Eldridge, J.E.T. (1972) *"Max Weber"* (London: Nelson)

Enelow J.M. and McGinnis M.D. (1989) *The Location of American Presidential Candidates: An Empirical Test of a New Spatial Model of Elections* " in Johnson P.E. (1989) *Formal Theories of Politics: Mathematical Modelling in Political Science* (Oxford: Pergamon Press)

Eve, R.A, Horsfall, S and Lee, M.E. (eds) (1997) *"Chaos, Complexity and Sociology: Myths, Models and Theories"* (London: Sage)

Feld, Grofman & Miller, (1989) *"Limits on Agenda Control in Spatial Voting Games"*, in Johnson, P.E. (1989) *"Formal Theories of Politics: Mathematical Modelling in Political Science"* (Oxford: Pergamon)

Gleick, J. (1988) *"Chaos: Making a New Science"* (New York: Penguin)

Gradstein, M. and Nitzam, S. (1989) *"Advantageous Multiple Rent Seeking"*, in Johnson, P.E. (1989) Formal Theories of Politics (Oxford: Pergamon)

Griffin, D., Shaw, P. and Stacey, R. (1998) *"Speaking of Complexity in Management Theory and Practice"*, in Organisation Vol.5, No.3, pp.315-339

Habermas, J (1984) *The Theory of Communicative Action: Volume I* (Boston: Beacon)

Hall, N, (1991) *"The New Scientist Guide to Chaos"* (Harmondsworth: Penguin)

Heisenberg (1969*) "Der Teil und das Ganze"* (Munich: R. Piper & Co.)

Holmes, B. (1981) *"Comparative Education: Some considerations of Method"* (London: Allen and Unwin)

Ingberman D.E. (1989) *Reputational Dynamics in Spatial competition* (Johnson P.E. 1989)

Kandel, I (1954) *"The New Era in Education: A Comparative Study"* (London: George Harrap)

Kant, I. (1993) *"Critique of Practical Reason"* (Upper Saddle River: Prentice Hall)

Koestler, A. (1964) *"The Sleepwalkers"* (Harmondsworth: Penguin)

Kuhn, T.S. (1962) *"The Structure of Scientific Revolutions"* (Chicago: University of Chicago Press)

Lauglo, J. & McLean, M. (1985) *"The Control of Education: International Perspectives on the Centralization/ Decentralization Debate"* (London: Heinemann Educational)

Maguire, S. and McKelvey, B. (1999) *"Complexity and Management: Moving from Fad to Firm Foundations"* in Emergence, Vol.1, No.2, pp.5-49 (www.emergence.org/Emergence/Contents12.html)

Martin, M.O. (2000) *"TIMSS 1999 International Science Report: Findings from IEA's Repeat of the Third International Mathematics and Science Study at the Eighth Grade"* (Chestnut Hill, MA: International Study Center, Lynch School of Education, Boston College)

McNiff (1992) *"Action Research: Principles and Practice"* (Lodnon: Routledge)

Mill, J.S, (1970) *"A System of Logic"* (London: Longman)

Morgan, G. (1997) *"Images of Organisation"* (London: Sage)

Mortimore, P, (1998) *"The Road to Improvement: Reflections on School Effectiveness"* (Lisse: Swets & Zeitlinger)

Mullis, I.V.S. (2000) *"TIMSS 1999 International Mathematics Report: Findings from IEA's Repeat of the Third International Mathematics and Science Study at the*

Eighth Grade" (Chestnut Hill, MA: International Study Center, Lynch School of Education, Boston College)

NCREL (2002) *"Action Research"* (www.ncrel.org/sdrs/areas/issues/envrnmnt/drugfree/sa3act.htm)

NERF (2000) *"Quality of Educational Research: Sub-group Report"* (London: National Educational Research Forum) also available at www.nerf-uk.org/documents/quality_report.pdf

Passerini, E, and Bahr, D (1997) *"Collective Behavior Following Disasters: A Cellular Automaton Model"* in Eve, R.A., Horsfall, S and Lee, M.E. (eds.) (1997) Chaos, Complexity and Sociology: Myths, Models and Theories (London: Sage)

Peaker, G (1971) *"The Plowden Children Four Years Later"* (London: NFER)

Plowden, (1967) *"Children and their Primary Schools: a Report of the Central Advisory Council for Education (England)"* (Also known as The Plowden Report) (London: HMSO)

Pratt, J. and Hillier, Y. (1991) *"New Funding Mechanisms in Higher Education: Bidding for Funds in the PCFC Sector"* (London: University of London Institute of Education)

Robitaille, D.F. and Garden, R.A. (1989) *"The Study of Mathematics II: Contexts and Outcomes of School Mathematics"* (Oxford: Pergamon)

Shavelson, R.J. and Towne, L. (2002) *"Scientific Research in Education"* (Washington, D.C.: National Academy Press)

Shotter, J. (1993) *"Cultural Politics of Everyday Life"* (Buckingham: Open University Press)

Thomas, G. (2002) *"Theory's Spell – On Qualitative Inquiry and Educational Research"*, British Educational Research Journal, Vol.28, No.3, pp.419-434

Thomas, G. (1997) *"What's the Use of Theory?"* Harvard Educational Review, Vol.67, No.1, pp.75-105

Tooley, J. (1998) *"Educational Research: A Critique"* (London: Ofsted)

Travers, K.J. and Westbury, I. (1989) *"The IEA Study of Mathematics I: Analysis of Mathematics Curricula"* (Oxford: Pergamon)

Tsoukas, H. (1998) *"Introduction: Chaos, Complexity and Organisation Theory"*, in Organisation Vol.5, No.3, pp.291-313

Turner, D.A. and Pratt, J. (1990) *"Bidding for Funds in Higher Education"*, in Higher Education Review, Vol.20, No.3, pp.19-33

Turner, D.A. (1992*) "Education and Chaos"*, in Higher Education Review Vol.25, No.1, pp.76-81

Turner, D.A. & Pratt, J. (1995) *"Funding Polytechnics in England: An Application of Non-linear Programming"* Socio-Economic Planning Science Vol.29.no.4, pp315-324

Index

16

16 plus, 88-90

A

achievement, 23, 64
action research, 16, 37, 62
ADHD, 16
agency, 8, 24, 29, 70, 80, 91, 149, 174, 181, 183
agent, 6, 63, 77, 152
Alisch, Azizighanbari and Bargfeldt, 175, 197
Althusser, 67, 69, 71
Archer, 40, 77, 103, 143, 183, 191, 194, 197
Armitage and Smith, 113
Arrow, 147-149, 159, 177
attainability, 109-115, 128, 132, 134
autonomy, 78, 97, 102, 105, 108, 143, 147, 161

B

baseball, 82, 179
Bassey, 43, 90, 197
BERA, 1
bidding, 124-125, 127, 131, 133-137, 150-151, 158
Blake, 37
Boudon, 80, 197
Boyle, 17, 73
butterfly effect, 159, 171-172, 174, 178

C

cash recovery, 133, 136, 138
chaos theory, 32, 70-71, 152-153, 159, 161-164, 171, 174-183
Charles, 17

chess, 81
class, 8, 11, 13, 23, 26-27, 33, 41-42, 44, 60-61, 70, 87-89, 94, 96, 110, 145, 149, 160, 162, 166, 192
classroom, 27, 45, 59, 61, 71, 143-146, 159, 162, 169, 175, 179
common sense, 19, 21, 44, 57, 63, 69, 74, 189
comparative education, 99, 104, 118
complexity theory, 161, 164, 173, 183
Comte, 15, 197
constraints, 103-104, 107, 109, 111, 112, 114-118, 120, 143
correlation, 46, 49, 89
creativity, 68, 71, 72

D

Data Envelope Analysis, 120
Davenport, 85-86, 198
Department for Education and Skills, 53, 59
dependent variable, 38, 40-42, 49
downward conflation, 77, 103, 143
dyslexia, 9, 22

E

Einstein, 21, 172
emergence, 164-165, 180, 183, 199

F

family background, 42
farmers, 91-93
fee only students, 130
Feyerabend, 67, 73
fisherman, 85-86
fractals, 169, 173
free will, 8-9, 11-13, 24, 29, 31, 43, 79, 80, 95, 161, 188-189, 193-194
freedom, 9-10, 108, 180, 183
Froebel, 71
fuzzy generalisations, 43, 90

G

Galileo, 19
game against nature, 78, 87
Game Against Nature, 85
game theory, 25, 29, 31-32, 43, 51, 70-71, 77-84, 88-96, 102, 143-144, 146-147, 157, 161, 177-179, 182-183
GCSE, 46, 87
General Teaching Council, 54
generalities, 70, 75
Germany, 112
Gleick, 163, 198
grand narrative, 67, 75, 187
grand theory, 67, 73-75
Griffin, Shaw and Stacey, 174

H

Habermas, 36, 193, 198
Hall, 163, 198, 199
handicap, 38, 39
Hawthorn, 188
Holmes, 99, 101-102, 199
homosexuality, 22
Hooke, 17-18, 73
Hooke's Law, 17-18, 73
humanism, 183
Hume, 40

I

IEA, 23, 38-39, 197, 199, 201
independent variable, 38, 40, 41, 43, 49
inputs, 103-104, 162
insurance level, 92

K

Kandel, 141, 199
Kant, 10-11, 24, 29, 40, 90, 199
Kuhn, 18-19, 63, 67, 72, 75, 187, 199

L

labelling, 8-9, 56, 68
laws, 16-17, 19, 24, 101-102

literature survey, 61

M

Maguire and McKelvey, 173-174, 180
maize, 91-92, 95
Mandelbrot Set, 165
matrix, 25, 27, 82-84, 86-88, 91, 96, 147
Mayo, 188
McNiff, 37, 55-58, 64, 194, 199
median voter, 151-153
method of differences, 35-36
method of similarities, 35-36
Mill, 35-36, 38, 44, 55, 58, 62, 64, 199
minimax, 85-86
mixed ability, 75
mixed strategy, 43, 83, 85-86, 90-93, 95, 97
moderation, 127-130, 133-134, 137-138
modernism, 185, 187, 189
Montessori, 71
Morgan, 169-170, 174, 178, 199
morphogenitic approach, 77
Mortimore, 45-49, 50, 52, 57, 64, 65, 194, 199
multi-centredness, 12, 90

N

National Research Council, 2, 6, 10
nature, 5, 20, 23, 25, 37-48, 58, 78, 86-87, 92, 96, 116-118, 146, 154, 156, 192, 194
NCDS, 87-88, 96
NERF, 1-2, 4-5, 200
Newton, 19, 37, 72-73, 192-193
Newtonian, 16, 63, 163, 173-176, 180, 182-183
non-zero sum, 25, 28
normal, 18-19, 23, 63, 72, 75, 80, 103, 117, 187

O

objective function, 103-104
Ofsted, 1, 201

operational research, 62, 78, 143
outputs, 103-104, 162

P

Pareto, 148-149, 157
Pareto optimal, 148-149, 157
partial autonomy, 12, 14, 31, 43, 46,
    48, 52, 64, 78, 95, 99, 146, 148-
    149, 161-163, 179-180, 183, 195
pathology of difference, 12
pay-off matrix, 25-26, 82, 87-88
PCFC, 123-124, 126-130, 134, 136,
    138, 140-141, 200
Peaker, 38-42, 44-45, 200
Pestalozzi, 71
Piaget, 71-72
policy, 3-5, 12-13, 16, 21, 32, 42, 44,
    49-50, 52, 59-60, 63, 65, 71, 74-
    75, 85, 91, 99-103, 105-107, 109,
    111-116, 118-120, 123-124, 125-
    129, 133-142, 146, 149, 152, 154-
    155, 157-158, 161, 166, 178
policy space, 106-107, 109, 111, 113-
    115, 119-120, 124, 126-129, 134-
    136, 152, 155, 157-158, 178
Popper, 40, 73, 99, 102
positivism, 15, 55
postmodernism, 16, 20, 67, 75, 192-
    193
practitioners, 3-5, 53, 62, 120
puzzle, 7, 18-19

R

recursive symmetry, 168-170, 181-
    182
regression, 38, 40-42, 44, 89, 90
Rogers, 32
routes, 12, 43, 51, 77, 79, 87

S

school effectiveness, 46-47, 49-50

school improvement, 46-47, 50
science, 1-2, 4-6, 14, 16, 18-19, 22,
    35, 37, 54-55, 62-64, 72-73, 75,
    93, 102, 160-161, 168, 176, 180,
    185-188, 190, 193-194
scientific revolutions, 18, 63
security level, 92
shadow price, 103, 116-117
Shotter, 174, 200
single-centredness, 11, 36, 43, 45-46,
    50, 52, 69, 75, 90, 97, 194
socialisation, 22-24, 146
sociological law, 99, 101-102, 117,
    119
Soviet Union, 23
strange attractor, 159, 170-172, 175-
    176, 178
sustainability, 112-115, 118, 132-137
systems thinking, 162

T

Teacher Training Agency, 53
Thomas, 67-71, 73-75, 194, 201
Tooley, 1-5, 21, 65, 74, 201
Tsoukas, 163-164, 180, 201
twins, 26-29, 31-32, 57, 61, 146

U

UFC, 124
UK, 1, 2, 8, 53, 103, 123, 154
United Kingdom, 13, 45, 79, 112, 139
upward conflation, 40, 77, 143
USA, 1-2, 6, 13, 78, 154
USSR, 23

W

Weber, 51, 81, 93, 198
will power, 6, 9, 188